THE BIG REVEAL

PART 1

AARON SMITH

Scrolls of Zebulon
Mobile, Alabama USA

Scrolls of Zebulon
P.O. Box 190309
Mobile, Alabama, USA
ScrollsOfZebulon.com
For inquiries, contact info@scrollsofzebulon.com

Throne Room Mountain diagram © 2019 by Elijah Ward
A Perpetual Room of Pathways of Chayei Olam diagram © 2019 by Joey Dixon

Cover and Interior Design by Sarah Smith
Photo of Aaron Smith by Jessica Fletcher
Edited by Rachel Hall and Teresa Bowen

ISBN: 978-1-7320203-3-7 (SC)

For Worldwide Distribution
Printed in the USA

Apostle F. Nolan & Shirley Ball

I dedicate The Big Reveal to F. Nolan Ball. His resilient heart and determined obedience to go where no man has gone enabled many great things to finish and greater works to begin. I attribute him as one who brought about the finishing of the Levitical order of the priesthood. By doing this, the cycles of the ages are broken and now the Zadok priesthood has become a reality.

He exemplified the strength and willingness to be a pioneer in walking out the revelation of the five-fold ministry. Because of F. Nolan Ball's steadfastness, Yahweh gave him His Hebrew names to be reintroduced back into the earth that enable the cycles of death to be broken.

He is now part of the great cloud of witnesses bearing witness of the truth in Heaven as it is on Earth. GLORY!

Apostle F. Nolan Ball (Nov. 14, 1929 - June 19, 2018)

TABLE OF CONTENTS

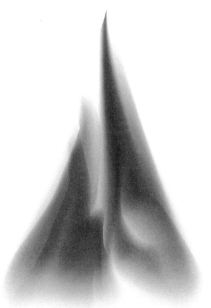

INTRODUCTION

While in the process of writing *Come Up Here*, my previous (and first) book, I knew that more was to follow. I didn't want to think about it, though, because the book was difficult to complete since all the pieces to the publishing puzzle were not yet in place. Scrolls of Zebulon was birthed from my needs and those of my associate, Teresa Bowen, for a publishing house that would not take the heart out of the prophetic process but would still produce high quality, well-edited books.

There has been an amazing response to our books from around the world, which has been surprisingly rewarding. I have written this book with great excitement and a deeper understanding of its potential to affect readers. I hope that *The Big Reveal* will prepare us all for what is upon us, and within us, by unveiling the purpose of what Yahweh desires to say.

If you have not read it yet, I encourage you to read *Come Up Here* before you delve into this book because understanding the culture of the Up Here is crucial.

Although this book is different than my first, it still carries the heart of the new dimensions in Yahweh. Here, I address the great changes that will be revealed on earth and in Heaven through the glory of Yahweh as it manifests in His family and creation. I also share personal stories to both keep you connected and take you somewhere as well. My endeavor, by the help of the Holy Ghost, is to nudge, shake, or make a shout to awaken us out of the slavery of Babylon and into the great glory of our Savior, Yahshua the Christ.

> [18] *For I reckon that the sufferings of this present time are not worthy to be compared with the glory which shall be revealed in us.* [19] *For the earnest expectation of the creature waiteth for the manifestation of the sons of God.* [20] *For the creature was made subject to vanity, not willingly, but by reason of him who hath subjected the same in hope,* [21] *Because the creature itself also shall be delivered from the bondage of corruption into the glorious liberty of the children of God.* [22] *For we know that the whole creation groaneth and travaileth in pain together until now.* (Rom. 8:18–22)

I am convinced that nothing will change in creation until we, His people, engage our scrolls. We must engage out of revelation and relationship—not from religious mindsets. When we are fully engaged, day in and day out, then the earth and all of creation will no longer groan, longing for its redemption and fulfillment. We will see its glorious redemption.

May the *chayei olam*, the everlasting life of Christ in us, be stirred and explode into greatness.

THE FIRST SIGNS

In 2006, based on a word she had heard, one of my associate ministers recommended that I read *Gold: The Once and Future Money* by Nathan Lewis.[1] Although I was more of a booklet man at the time, I trusted her word to be true. I have always enjoyed reading, but my attention to any distraction had kept me from finishing many expansive books I'd started. In somewhat of a protest, I eventually read the book—all of its 464 pages—but I didn't get what Yahweh intended for me to receive. However, I felt the conviction to properly honor the word given to me. So, I reread the book.

The second time, much of my reading was done on my knees. I mention that not to impress you, but to emphasize that I truly got the importance of this word to me, so much so that I honored it on my knees. It became a word of God to me and therefore holy. The second go-around worked: my

---

1 Hoboken, NJ: John Wiley & Sons, Inc., 2007.

eyes were opened to an ancient path leading to the future of the importance that gold plays in world economics.

At first, I thought God wanted me to reveal that the gold standard is the way to go, but He said: "Not so fast." Gold was, and still could, be a measuring rod that brings about equality and stability, but historically it was too slow to compete with fiat money. Fiat money is inconvertible paper money made legal tender by a government decree. The word *fiat*[2] means "authoritative sanction." *Fiat* is Latin and literally means "let it be done." In other words, let us decide what it is. This sounds familiar to how Babylon was created.[3]

From Lewis's book, I learned about the Bretton Woods system, the code of Hammurabi and other ancient exchange systems, including means of financial shrewdness such as fractional banking. I dug deep into these paths. Some of the ancient paths are still engaged today. Through my study of Lewis' book, God was teaching me some of the reasons for and effects of systems set up through man's continued choice to do things apart from Him. This remains the sad story of mankind as a whole attempting to live to themselves apart from their amazing creator.

When I was settling in on the gold standard as Yahweh's word to fix financial instability, He introduced another book to me. The brilliantly authored *Lords Of Finance: The Bankers Who Broke the World* presents the opposite view of the gold standard.[4] Liaquat Ahamed offers not just an attack of the gold standard, but a historical fact path of man's selfish and prideful

2 "Fiat" Dictionary.com Accessed April 29, 2019 https://www.dictionary.com/browse/fiat
3 In another chapter I will discuss Babylon and why it was created. The initial story is in Genesis 11.
4 Liaquat Ahamed. *Lords of Finance: The Bankers Who Broke the World.* New York: Penguin Press, 2009.

methods of manipulating the financial systems that affect us all. You may be thinking, "All?" Yes: *all*. Even a villager in a remote developing country who has never heard of any financial system is affected by the maneuvering of financial standards.

We are all affected financially through war. War is a global issue. It has affected us all, and war is hell: warriors describe it that way and much blood has been sadly and horrifically spilled onto this earth. This blood cries out to us for justice's sake. Wars are declared over a few universal issues (disputed territory rights, religious/cultural differences, desire for power, etc.), but the ability to wage a war always involves the strength to fund that war. I believe smaller countries that are well-funded can defeat larger ones.[5] This is a natural order[6] and is true, except when it comes into conflict with spiritual laws our Father Yahweh has put into place. He has always made a way of escape through His dimensional realms of faith.

In his 576-page account, Ahamed cites four central bankers for many horrible outcomes in the early to mid-20th century. Ahamed argues that the First World War, World War II, and the stock market crash of 1929 that precipitated the Great Depression were a result of the actions of these four bankers. I highly recommend reading Ahamed's and Lewis's books. They will give you an idea of some of what Yahweh revealed to me through these men's ideas. For example, even good ideas like the gold standard will not work without Yahweh. He holds the only plan and it will work when His family is in charge. We,

---

5   Ranker.com. Remember David in 1 Sam. 17 when they are fighting for a cause.
6   A popular comic strip, *The Wizard of Id*, created by Brant Parker and Johnny Hart, illustrates the principle when the tyrannical King reminds his people, "We must all live by The Golden Rule." What is that rule? "Whoever has the gold makes the rules." It originally appeared May 3, 1965.

His family, will lead gloriously and majestically with mercy and truth.

Shocks at Saks

In the winter of 1998, my wife and I, along with a couple from our church, visited New York City in celebration of my wife's 40th birthday. Our plans included visiting the typical sightseeing attractions and catching a few Broadway plays. It was almost Christmas, so along with seeing The Rockettes at Radio City Music Hall, shopping was on the schedule.

The shopping was different from what I was used to in Mobile, Alabama. We went into Saks Fifth Avenue to pick up on a few sales. It was the day of the sweater sale and we walked in just in time to engage with a table full of designer sweaters. Wow! Everyone was at it like piranhas, so I jumped in. It was a half-off sale, so I grabbed me a cashmere beauty. I was overjoyed until I saw the sale price: $500.00. I gently put the sweater back into the dwindling pile. It barely touched the table before someone with undoubtedly better finances than me grabbed it. I thought, "Oh, well." We rarely wear sweaters in Mobile, so who was going to see it anyway? The price-points were a shock to us all and we realized that we were way out of our league.

I guess the look on my face was obvious because one of the store's personnel working behind a nearby counter invited me to look at the men's ties. They were all carefully folded in the well-lit display. He laughed and said, "You think those prices are ridiculous?" He guided me to one particular tie. He said, "Take a guess at the price of this baby." It was $1,300.00! It had gold thread in it, and he told me, "Someone will actually buy it one day." The tie wasn't pretty to me, but I agreed with him that someone will buy it—but only for a status symbol. I have realized for some time that there is plenty of money in the world—but it needs to get into the hands of the righteous.

We decided to leave our future shopping trips to Macy's or other more moderately priced stores. But first we went up to Saks' fifth floor to dine in the beautiful restaurant. We walked into the elaborate foyer with its grand marble entrance and crystal chandelier. We knew the prices would be expensive and were preparing to look at the menus placed on a stand near the entrance, but we didn't get that far. While waiting our turn for the host, we spotted a large rat, about 8 inches in body length along with the usual ugly tail. He strolled his way across the elegant shiny floor. That thing was huge. To our surprise, no one but us spotted him. We exited Saks. We found a great little pizza place and I devoured one of the best pizzas I've ever had—for a very reasonable price.

Vision on the NYSE Trading Floor

After lunch, our friends wanted to see the financial district in lower Manhattan. We visited the World Trade Centers first. We had no idea that in less than three years those two huge buildings would crumble to the ground. Continuing our tour of the business district, we found our way to the New York Stock Exchange. We signed up for the standard tour of a view of the trading floor to see the trading pods and all the traders in their different colored vests scrambling around. While standing in line behind the building waiting for our tour to start, Yahweh plainly tapped me on my shoulder. He said to watch and listen, for He desired to show me something.

We ascended up the elevators to a holding area. There, the guide separated the large group into smaller groups of fifty. The group we were in was too large. So, the kind lady asked the four of us to stay behind and said she would let us go in by ourselves between groups. Perfect.

We were able to go in and view the trading floor by ourselves. While there, I told my wife and friends that Yahweh was about to speak to me, and they politely gave me some space.

Standing in the middle of the viewing platform, I observed the room and several things stood out to me. First, on the opposite wall from us, a huge poster read: "The World Puts Its Stock in Us." I looked to my right where a huge American flag hung on the wall. I looked to my left and saw another huge American flag on the wall, just over the platform with the trading bell and gavel. On the floor below were the trading pods.

Suddenly, from my right, a massive gold flaming sword came through the wall, through the American flag, then went through the ceiling. It continued through the wall to my left, passing all the way through the other American flag, the podium, and finally into the floor. As it disappeared into the floor, it created a two-foot wide crevasse all the way across the room. A vacuum formed, sucking everything in the room into the huge opening. Then it quickly closed up. When it closed, a wadded up piece of paper rolled to the side. I stood in awe.

I asked Yahweh what I had just witnessed. He said that what the NYSE floor represents is held together by only one Word. Upon release of that Word, all of it goes away in an instant. The wadded up piece of paper was a symbol of the only remains of something that at one time existed. Then He said that 2007 and 2008 would be the great exchange, yet the great exchange would only be a setup for the greater exchange that would begin in a much different way at the end of 2017 and be fully engaged during 2018.

The Crash/The Great Exchange

In 2007 and 2008, when the financial system was collapsing, I recognized that, in the vision I had at the NYSE during our vacation in 1998, I had spiritually discerned the time of the great exchange. My prophetic team and I failed, though, to know what to do about it. Some skilled in the financial world saw the bubble, but even the majority of financial experts missed it. It's difficult to believe now, but at that time we were not yet engaged with the Seven Spirits of the Lord found in Isaiah 11:2.

> ...[T]he spirit of the Lord shall rest upon him, the spirit of wisdom and understanding, the spirit of counsel and might, the spirit of knowledge and of the fear of the Lord.

We had not been invited to engage with them yet because we were still in the ages of war. I'm sure they were available for some people, as the Seven Spirits of the Lord are eternal, but we had not received the invitation to engage with them yet. The ages of peace began in 2009 for us. In that amazing year, great and wonderful change came as we began to awaken to our purpose.

One Monday in 2008, as we were realizing the crash, it appeared to be the end of business and life as we knew it at that time. I still have cold, heavy, horrific feelings of *Oh, no!*

that remind me of the horror of that day. I pastor the small but close-knit church family at The Rock of Mobile. At different times on that Monday morning, four dedicated men came to see me in my office. The news from each was that their businesses were going to fail. It was heart-wrenching for them and to our small church, not to mention that they were our top-givers as far as dollar amounts go. Logically, it looked bad. Then, in that unbelievable moment, Yahweh spoke to me ever so gently and confidently. He said, "Go into your conference room for I want to reveal to you something." I thought He would give me a strategy of how to pray for the hurting people and the wisdom to offer them about how to make it.

He said, "It's time to connect the dots." I thought He was using an analogy, but He meant it literally. I asked about the hurting people. I felt I needed to do something more for them. He said everything would be alright to those who put their trust in Him.

The men lost their businesses and went through some tough times. At this point, all but one have regained great businesses and are doing well. The one decided on another route. His heart was too offended to move on with us. I only heard from him a couple of times early on after the collapse. He disappeared into the world—and that is his right. The others are determined to stay in position, and it will pay off for them. They are the world-changers. How so? They will be some of the first to experience the big reveal, for they are part of it. They will have choice seats because they didn't run when it would have been easy in some ways to do so. Everyone has a right to quit, but it is an expensive decision—that is, if they want Yahweh's greatness.

Connecting the Dots

When Yahweh said to connect the dots, He gave me specifics. Remember, horror was going on just outside my doors. I felt that I should be actively assisting those facing disaster and hurting, but God called me away to something that seemed irresponsible. Yet, He does know best. Do we really believe that He knows best? Of course we do, but sometimes our actions are more reactions than engaging Him and His Word. Yahweh gave me instructions to get a poster board and colored pencils. Although they knew of the looming disasters facing some of our people, my assistants still manned their stations. There are a number of artists in my church for whom I am grateful. They provided me with a cream-colored poster board and a professional-quality multi-colored pencil set. I had more colors at hand than I knew existed. I sat privately in my conference room and had waited only for a moment when Yahweh asked, "Do you see the first dot?"

I didn't at first. He encouraged me to keep looking. My mind was challenging me, but I finally zoned out and engaged in the moment. I kept looking. Then, to my left, on the poster board I saw a small dot. Immediately Yahweh said to color it a particular color. He then said to make the dot bigger, circle the dot with another color, and repeat it a second time. A total of three separate, concentrically aligned colors created the dot.

Then He asked if I saw the next dot. Suddenly, I saw the second one. It was made up of different colors than the first. Then I saw a third, and so on. I knew there was a pattern to the dots, but I couldn't see it yet. He kept asking me over and over, "Do you see it?" Finally, He presented me with another life-changing request. He said: "Come Up Here."

I stood in my chair. I looked down at the poster board I'd been drawing on. Lo and behold, there it was: the dots I had drawn made up a model of the wheel in the wheel described by Ezekiel (Ezek. 1 and 10) and Revelations 4. Yahweh showed me a mechanism in the center. With its eight faces, it was the shape of an octahedron. He said to turn it at a thirty- to thirty-five degree angle. (The octahedron can be turned thirty to thirty-five degrees, depending on the request.)

Wow! I know I just shifted gears on you here, but that is the way things suddenly changed for me. Yahweh began to teach me ancient secrets and the protocol for how this device (or whatever it was I was seeing—I didn't yet know) was to work. He told me that there are rules of order that must never change, for they are the governors. Following the rules of order provides evidence that His Kingdom is being honored. He also said that most mechanisms only require a few rules of order. Then, it is up to the eye of the creator in us to build what is there. Amazing!

Yahweh instructed me to name each one of the dots on the outside of the wheel. I named them from what I learned through Ahamed's and Lewis' books about the Babylonian financial system. I named the dots of the inside wheel from specific instructions Yahweh gave me concerning each dot. The dots of the inside wheel represented methods and ways which Yahweh would use in His Kingdom systems of justice.

Later, I learned that the dots were the tenth Hebrew letter, *Yud*, י. Yud is the beginning and finishing of Yahweh's thoughts and desires. Yud sets up the place for the spiral staircase of ascending and descending throughout the universe (*layil* and *luwl*). The dots—or yuds—were also portals of Yahweh's desired path to set up Babylon for its fall mentioned in Revelations 17–18.

This led me to two other Hebrew letters, *Ayin*, ‫ע‬, the sixteenth letter, and *Ghah*, ‫ﬡ‬, the twenty-third letter. In reference to what I had seen of the wheels in Ezekiel 1 and Ezekiel 10, the dots in the wheels were the eyes all around (see Ezek. 1:18, 10:12). Ayin is the eye or portal. Ghah is a letter that was taken out of the Hebrew Aleph-Beit while the Hebrews were held in Babylonian captivity. Ghah looks like two ropes twisted, but they represent the spiraling staircase mentioned above. The Hebrews removed the letter for mysterious reasons. You can find many published reasons for the letter's removal, but I believe it was removed because it represents an open path to a secret place. This secret place is called *Choshek*. While the Hebrews were held in captivity, they blended the letters Ghah and Ayin together to form the letter Ghayin. It was important to keep the letter. That it was later removed speaks to me of a potentially lost heart and thus a lost path. Let us remember that in John 14:6 Yahshua said, *"I am the way, the truth, and the life: no man cometh unto the Father, but by me."*

I am finding out that many of the duties still ahead of us and the path that we must become accustomed to is the path of *layil* and *luwl*. You first find our friends Layil and Luwl in Genesis 1:5, "And God called the light Day, and the darkness he called Night." *Night* is from the Hebrew *layil*. It has an associated word, *luwl*, that describes the depths of its being.

- Layil: Strong's H3915. The Hebrew word is ‫לַיִל‬, Lamed Yud Lamed. Its definition is "a twist (away of the light)."

- Luwl: Strong's H3883. The Hebrew word is לוּל, Lamed Vav Lamed. Its definition is "to fold back; a spiral step: winding stair."

This ancient path will lead us into the depths of *Ghah*. The mystery of Ghah can be interpreted in two ways. Ghah is described as the twisted rope. Some explain the twisting as wicked. Those who believe Ghah leads to a twisted and wicked path may be correct where they are coming from. However, I understand and see Ghah as the spiraling of light. This twisting of light is the path for those of us who hear the invitation from the Father to come Up Here. The Word in us from our Father calls us to ascend and descend with the Word in us from our Father. It leads those of us who see it as a lit trail to a place of discovery that holds secrets and mysteries of the fullness of the glory of all creation. We are the ones who can identify the reality of what is there and what its purpose is, for we are of our Father.

The First Wheel

Once I had collected the information to place on the portals of the wheels, I decided to build a physical model of what I was seeing. As I have mentioned, I have a great team who joined my vision and have made it like their own. It takes a dedicated, believing team to see a vision or dream become reality. I'm rich with believers and I am so thankful.

I have pastored for years and my church, though small in number, is great in ability. Every time I've needed expertise in an area, I usually have an expert in my church who fills the need. It is ordered of the Lord, for sure.

Mike Fletcher is one of those experts. I have known Mike since he was twelve years old. He and his family have been dedicated in our church since its beginning in 1990. His father, Ernie, became a close friend and served in many areas of helps ministry including the music ministry. Ernie played the trumpet. I recently heard one of his granddaughters playing his trumpet. It was amazing to watch her play. Ernie was diagnosed with leukemia in 1997 and passed in October of 2000, nine months after my mother had passed from breast cancer. It was a tough year, but we kept moving. Two days before Ernie passed, he called me to ask me to take care of his family. I have taken it seriously. Mike was his oldest child, and is now in his forties. Mike became an amazing math teacher who has been recognized locally as well as nationally. He coauthored a math textbook used in high school curriculums nationally. Ernie's other son, Joe, has been very successful with Verizon. He's been offered by top executives, a chance to move up in the company, but Joe sees the importance of family over career and has remained positioned here at home in Mobile. I'm thankful. Wendy is the youngest and has likewise remained steady and steadfast. They all three are raising loving and respectful children. I'm proud of them all. Jill, Ernie's wife, has remained here also and is now sixty-nine. Jill is an expert in a local health store. Loyalty is their word. All four of them are super-smart and use their skills for the Kingdom. I'm so thankful for them.

When Mike first heard what I was seeing and doing, he was enamored that I was looking into geometry and math. He knew I didn't have any formal education in either, so he knew what I was seeing had to be from God. Mike assisted in mathematical advice but was also was a sounding board for geometric protocol. When I began to notice shapes, primarily the five Platonic solids, Mike assured me in what I was seeing and has never acted threatened that someone like me, uneducated in math, can see this stuff. On the contrary, he celebrated what I was doing. When one of my assistants, Rachel Miller, revealed her skill in creating the wheels from model parts she made out of cardboard, Mike offered to help obtain better materials. He gave us a kit of Zometools, a type of construction set which provided the perfect materials designed exactly for what we wanted to build. Rachel was ecstatic.

One year before Yahweh gave me the call to build the wheels, Teresa Bowen, along with a group of prophetic musicians from our church, asked to give a prophetic music teaching. I agreed to give them a Wednesday night service. They gave a presentation on the circle of fifths. Along with the entire congregation, I didn't get it. But we love prophetic folks, so we honored their enthusiasm. I don't believe they understood it either, but the prophetic typically works that way. Usually, demonstration comes first, followed some time thereafter by revelation. Patience is definitely a virtue in these scenarios.

The day I realized we were building the wheels from Ezekiel 1, I was reminded of that service from one year earlier. I knew how we were to build the wheels from the understanding of the circle of fifths. The inside wheel was in minor chords while the outside wheel was in major chords— just like the order of the circle of fifths.

Yahweh began to teach me about what He calls "rules of

order." He gave me seven numbers to use to mark the wheel. The numbers were aligned with the seven musical chords from the key of A through the key of G. He then showed me a timing-piece to be placed in the center of the middle wheel. It was an octahedron with its eight faces and six vertices. This is when He began to teach me about dimensions. At this point, I realized I was creating a musical instrument. I had no idea at the time, but I was building a device that not only played a unique sound but it could create a pattern of algorithms. (Miraculous, I know!) Later I discovered what a big deal this would become.

The first wheel had a specific purpose. I say "first wheel" but at the time I thought it would be the only one. It was so special that I didn't think I could come up with another one. Later on, two of my friends challenged me: if I could find the first one, then I could find the other three. They were correct. With much help, I did. The minute they challenged me, I could see it. Eventually, I embraced it.

In building the first wheel, I had to set a pattern that I knew the other wheels would follow. But they all would be uniquely different from each other. The first wheel's purpose was to perform three things. I can divulge two of the three, but one of them remains a secret until the dimensions of greatness appear.

Purpose: Identification of Those Who Engage

The first purpose of the wheel was to identify those of us who would engage with it. We engaged with the wheel through inputting specific information about our lives (our given names and our home addresses) that made us different from each other. We used our given names and our home addresses. This occurred in the days prior to much revelation of the ages. The Seven Thunders had not been given yet. We didn't engage with Eber yet—we didn't even know he existed.

Before the process could work, Yahweh had a prophet from another city call us. She said we were missing something in the center of the wheels. She said that we would find the secret in downtown Mobile, near or in Fort Conde. Wow! A treasure hunt followed.

I took a small prophetic group to Fort Conde. Fort Conde is a museum now, but years ago it was a bastion of protection for the city. It was initially built by the French around 1720. Years later, it fell into the hands of the British, and then to the Spanish. Finally, it was claimed by the United States. At Fort Conde, we began to look for something that only our eyes of the spirit could spot. We looked everywhere for something that would speak to us. When we were near giving up, about to leave, and ready to reconsider the word we'd been given, Holy Ghost whispered mysteriously to look to my right.

On the wall was a map of the fort. I had been to the top of the fort and couldn't see it from that vantage point, but the overview map made it clear: the fort was shaped like a key. I knew instantly that was what we were looking for.

When you are making something tangible that has been held in darkness for ages, you don't rush it. The process to build the wheels has been meticulous. When we would attach something wrong to the model, or put something in a wrong place on the wheel, our eyes of the spirit immediately knew something was off. In a way, it is the same process an artist critiquing her own painting or a sculptor evaluating his sculpture in progress goes through—you just know. That was the case for us.

When we discovered the map which revealed the key, I began to see dimensions that it was to unlock. I began to realign Heaven and earth. One of my associates understands the constellations, and Yahweh gave me an understanding of the elements of the earth.[7] We discovered that the key was to be inserted into the octahedron, and the shape would transform to reveal the specific alignment patterns of the constellations and elements. Every component was numbered and colored for its frequency.

Purpose: Identifying Yahweh's Economics

The second purpose of the first wheel is that it aids in observing and understanding the economics of Babylon and in perceiving Yahweh's economic plan. There is much more to it than that simple explanation, but the way it works in this purpose is similar to the way we used it for our names. We first built the wheels by hand, but there came a time when Yahweh said to put them into a computerized, animated graphic form. I wasn't excited about getting a computer involved and didn't know anyone that could do it. I also didn't have the money to fund it.

I asked around for a while to those I knew were tech-savvy, but no one had this type of skill. The youngest of our four children, Joshua, volunteered to learn. He did after some time of study and financial investment—as a matter of a fact, he did very well. We sent him to a high-tech language school in Reston, Virginia. At the time of this writing, Joshua is thirty,

---

7 I will share in more detail in Part 2 of what we have discovered of the constellations and the elements.

but at the time, he was in his early twenties. He had already discovered he enjoyed the tech world through photography. His photography teacher was an older professional gentleman who encouraged him to pursue digital photography. The field was new at the time. Joshua adhered to his mentor's advice and began to engage with the digital world. He found he was designed for it.

Joshua wasn't interested in school growing up and his grades reflected his lack of interest. It was a struggle to get him through our private Christian school. We still have the school and Joshua is now an advisor on our board as we endeavor to find a new way of doing school. Joshua's experience provided some of our motivation to change.

Joshua now heads up the technology for the company we started called OPe. He, along with his good friend and one of my spiritual sons, Chad McCollum, lead the technology for a light-based encryption chip. Chad also graduated from our school. Our technology operates in the nano and microscopic scale and we guide photons with this technology to encrypt data. Amazing. This all is made possible by the algorithms of the four wheels, but it started with Joshua learning how to create computer graphics.

As Joshua learned how to create graphics for the first wheel and as we engaged with it, I began to see definable patterns. I put together a team of people whom I believed were those who can see and hear by the spirit. I asked for anyone in our church interested in what I was doing to come to a special gathering where I would input their names into the wheel. (I have a very special group of people who love what Yahweh loves. How many churches can do this? Not many, and I'm thankful for those who love me enough to believe with me.)

We input over one hundred people's names into what we had learned from the wheel. The graphics weren't ready yet, so we manually connected the sounds and dots. Y.A. Butler played them on the piano (she's a seer at the Rock of Mobile and a coauthor for *Friends of Eber*). As she played in the pattern of the circle of fifths, I had the seers listen and watch for the sounds of the individual. We created their new sounds and the colors of their identity from this dimension. We matched the frequencies of color with their sound. Each one was like a fingerprint of their individuality.

It was only the beginning—but it was awesome.

The Second Wheel

The first wheel was well on its way when I began to engage with Holy Ghost about the second wheel. The second wheel is primarily concerned with the wholeness of our physical bodies. What is so interesting to think about is that this occurred before the revelation of *chayei olam*, everlasting life. The way I saw it was that the first wheel would play the sound of whomever's information was input into it, and that sound would awaken the second wheel.

The second wheel was the same size and the same shape as the first, and its colors aligned with the colors of the first wheel. The first big difference in the second wheel is that, once it joined to play in unison with the sound of the first wheel, it began to transform. The second wheel would transform into five different shapes before it finished its adjustment. Basically, as it transforms, it rewrites the music to the original sound that the cells of our bodies identify from our original scrolls or physical creation. That original sound isn't attached to the curse of being tethered to the sun and moon. The second wheel makes a frequency of the sound that the cells within our bodies will awaken to. It isn't attached to the law of a seed but to the Word of Yahweh from the original intent.

When I first looked at the model of the second wheel that was eventually hanging on the wall of my conference room, I saw that it too had a wheel within the wheel. I thought that the inner wheel would be perfect to place the design of the double helix of molecules of nucleic acids known as DNA. I began my research on DNA coding with a team of researchers and the file of what we found became huge. I looked up all the primary diseases known to man and began to correlate them to the thirty-nine stripes upon Yahshua's body found in scripture. I thought I was on to something, but the voice of Yahweh was suddenly silent. We had accumulated files and files of information. I thought that this second wheel could take years of research. I finally decided to ask why Yahweh was so silent.

He said to look up all of the possibilities of different things going on in one living cell. I did: I found the information stored in one cell could hold as many as 3 billion different possibilities. "This could take a while," was my initial thought. Yahweh said, "Let us do it another way."

Any other way sounded better than the path I was on. He said, "Let us use just five things." Just five things? That was awesome! He said that He had created everything with five things in mind. Light, sound, shapes, color, and numbers were His five basic creative paths.

Entering the Nano Dimension

I have been in association with scientists for some time now and I've learned to look from their eyes on some things. I know that color comes from refracted light and that shapes help form the refractions. Color itself serves to identify what is there. It's part of something's identity. The color found on insects was once thought to come from physical pigmentation. This understanding began to change when Yahweh allowed man to begin to discover the nano world. Scientists have discovered that at the nano scale, the skin or shell-like covering of an insect or reptile is made up of designs which refract light.[8] The colors respond the same way as a rainbow. Reflected and refracted light from the shapes allows the numbering of designs and lines on their bodies.

＊　＊　＊

One day before my encounter with the dots, I was in my office looking out my window. I was waiting for something, but I didn't know what. I felt out of touch: I was a minister responsible to take care of the people Yahweh had given me to help and pray for, and here I was studying world economics. I knew my study was the word of the Lord to me—I was confident of that—but nothing appeared to be happening from it. As I looked out my window, I said I felt like I was watching grass grow. Everything appeared to be going so slow. I felt irresponsible.

Yahweh gave me a challenge that I'll never forget. He said, "Study what happens when grass is growing." Me and my

8 Laura Geggel. "Chameleons' Color-Changing Secret Revealed." LiveScience. March 10, 2015. Accessed March 27, 2019. https://www.livescience.com/50096-chameleons-color-change.html.

big mouth, I thought—but it began an amazing journey that I remain on to this day. Through my study of grass growing, He began to teach me about fractals. Nothing that He created was randomly designed. He introduced me to the nano world which I now love so much.

＊ ＊ ＊

I have had the distinct pleasure and honor of becoming friends with Dr. Paul Joseph, the principal scientist at the Institute for Electronics and Nanotechnology (IEN) at Georgia Tech in Atlanta, Georgia. Dr. Joseph was initially a cancer research scientist, and he's originally from India. I was instructed by business people not to let anyone in academia know that I was a pastor, so I was incognito—or so I thought.

When I first met Dr. Joseph, he and I discussed the nano dimension, or scale, as scientists call it. As he and I discussed the different scales of this very small world, he began to describe the peculiar ways of the nano dimension. He described how the microscopic dimension has distinct differences from the nano dimension. The nanoscale has only been discovered for a few decades because it is so small: a nanometer is one-billionth of a meter. As he began to describe one big difference, I noticed an amazing aura around him. He looked and sounded different than many of the scientists I had met. I thought, "Could he be a believer?" But I was very cautious not to bring the subject up. This man was like the gatekeeper to this place and it appeared OPe needed to do our work there.

Dr. Joseph explained that when we peer into and touch the microscopic world, it is affected by our presence and is easily manipulated. Except, he said, it is not so in the nano world.

Scientists move things around in the nano world for the sake of observation, and the things in the nano world respond by correcting themselves back to their original design. The nano world, he explained, is a very orderly world, and it is beautiful. Scientists have just barely touched the surface there of all that is to be discovered.

The way Dr. Joseph described this dimension sounded to me just like the way the family of God would describe it. I still didn't reveal who I really was, but soon he picked up on something. We were headed to lunch when he asked what else I do. Well, here we go. I said, "I pastor a church in Mobile." He lit up and asked me if I was denominational or nondenominational. I immediately responded with "Nondenominational," and he said "Me, too." He explained that he is a fourth-generation Christian from India. Years ago missionaries visited the area where his family is from and many were saved.

I was moved to tears for many reasons. I was thinking of the faithful missionaries who I'm sure had no idea that one of the great-grandsons of the people they had led into the Kingdom would go on to do such great things as Dr. Paul Joseph. If I had dared think about his name when I first met him, I might have picked up that he was a brother in Christ. I was greatly moved that Yahweh had so ordered our steps.

Dr. Joseph and I have become good friends and I share with him whatever is on my heart spiritually. He has spoken in our church and it was awesome! When I shared the vision for OPe with him, he said that he would help with whatever he could. He said that God really does have everything under control and has people in many places we wouldn't think possible.

Dr. Joseph told me about one of his friends, Dr. James Tour, a synthetic organic chemist who specializes in nanotechnology and is based at Rice University in Houston, Texas. He builds nanocars.[9] Dr. Joseph invited Dr. Tour to come to Georgia Tech and give a talk on his nanocars and nanobots. He said he would, but he needed the liberty to share the gospel, too. Of course, Dr. Joseph obliged him.

Before he came, Dr. Tour sent his posters to be posted on campus. The title of his talk was "Nanocars and Jesus Christ." The response to register was so large that they had to use the largest auditorium. When the day of the talk came, the place was packed. Dr. Tour spoke first for about thirty minutes on the astounding accomplishments of what his team had learned and created in nanobots and nanocars. Dr. Tour continued to speak, saying, "Now if you desire to know how we have attained such knowledge, you have to meet the one that introduced it to us and guided us into it." Dr. Joseph said he was amazed at not only the boldness of Dr. Tour, but at how no one left the room when he began to preach. Astonishing!

Yahweh's plan is intact. He has said, *"For I know the plans I have for you, …plans to prosper you and not to harm you, plans to give you hope and a future"* (Jer. 29:11).[10]

Destination: Eradicating Disease

Some of the future technology that Yahweh has given us through OPe will be with nanobots. We plan to go after cancer

---

9   "Rice University Richard E. Smalley Institute for Nanoscale Science and Technology." Trynano.org. February 05, 2016. Accessed March 27, 2019. http://trynano.org/organizations/rice-university.
10   I Googled this verse and someone's website claimed this verse is taken out of context if used personally. How sad to have such a religious and confined mind. Of course it is valid for me now, for the word of God is living. If they measure everything by this pattern then they have nothing to stand on. (Pardon my soapbox.)

and other horrific diseases via the nano dimension. Dr. Joseph is primarily a cancer research scientist. He explains that in the nano dimension, cancer can't hide. Healthy cells are smooth and beautiful while cancerous corrupt cells are bumpy and ugly. The numbers tell on the corrupt cells by revealing their location.

A friend and business partner of mine, Dr. Barry Morgan, took me to visit a premier cancer hospital just outside of Atlanta. I had a brief chat with one of their primary physicians. I asked if they do anything with nanobots. He quickly said, "No," explaining that technology isn't smart enough yet and he didn't see it doing much in the near future. From his perspective, there is nothing to out-perform the knife. That is sad.

My mother was sixty-one when cancer claimed her life. What a nightmare it was. She was cut up and filled with poison, then burned up with radiation. The treatment was barbaric. Advancements have been made since that time, and for that I'm thankful, but that experience is now a part of my motivation in all that I do in this arena. We have been given the foundation for technology that will eliminate the knife, poisonous chemicals, and the use of photons to burn up not only cancer but healthy tissue and cells. With a full crew of scientists who will be free to overcome sickness and disease, we are at the door of a breakthrough to enter this field.

I've had many questions regarding why we would head down a path that could extend not just life but also wickedness. When I enquired of the Lord concerning this matter, His quick response was that He loves us and everlasting life is a gift from Him and not man in their wisdom. This may bring up many issues to challenge utopian thinking that only the righteous can be healed. That is not the purpose here, I assure you. Yahweh is wisdom and He has sent the Spirit of Wisdom to assist us in revealing Yahweh's heart. The answer to eradicating disease should come from us and not from some lawless system of the rich who exemplify Babylon and call it philanthropy. In reality, the whole earth belongs to Yahweh and He loves the entire world.[11]

When the first wheel played the tune of the individual to awaken the second wheel, it played the sound three times. Then the second wheel transformed into the shape of a nautilus shell to honor the golden ratio of 1.618. Most everything in natural creation fits the golden ratio. All of the assigned numbers produced from the music of the first wheel would be placed in five compartments for organization. These five groups then would be placed on the next transformer of a wheel-like shape that had every note from the circle of fifths. The groups of notes and numbers were specifically placed on the spoke- or prong-like shapes on the second wheel to begin allowing it to rewrite the song for the body.

While I am leaving many details out, I'm trying to give you a picture that the procedure is not random, but detailed and orderly. Once the letters or chords were properly placed on the second wheel, then they would be released and ascend into a train-like perfectly aligned pattern. At this point the letters would reattach to the wheel within the wheel and your

---

11 There will be more on this subject in Part 2 of *The Big Reveal.*

original sound would begin to play. The second wheel would then harmonize with the first wheel.

The Third Wheel

While in harmony, the first and second wheels align to direct their sounds toward the third wheel to awaken it. The third wheel is about the mind and the brain and their capacity to receive the Christ-mind. Oracle Teresa Bowen saw a crystalline lattice cover spiraling and covering the wheel of the mind. When the two wheels sang or played to the third wheel, the lattice cover removed itself so the light and sounds could connect to the wheel.[12]

As the third mind wheel began to awaken, just as the other two, it formed into a similar wheel within a wheel. Then all three played the identity sound from the first wheel in unison. Hearing the sound of your identity is the first event that aligns you to your path. While the second wheel had its own sound now, it played the identity sound from the first wheel, too. The purpose of the first and second wheel playing in unison was to awaken the third wheel. The mind wheel did not know its own sound yet, but, once awakened, it played the identity sound three times through the circle of fifths scale. Then, somewhat like the second wheel, it began to transform. The third wheel transformed three times. Once it began to transform, it first became a cube. The cube represents the six faces of all knowledge, from all four corners, and the up and down.

---

12 Teresa also saw the mind wheel had to be the second wheel, but that is not the order Yahweh gave to me. I get what she is saying, and that may be how the wheels operate when all four are in place, but my order was the identity wheel first, followed by the health wheel, and the mind wheel third.

Visible Effects of Frequency

When we began to engage with what the cube from the third wheel was all about, I did a study on sound frequency. The physical designs of the frequencies of sound are truly amazing. They look like shapes from some alien form. The study of the shapes resulting from the patterns of sound is called cymatics. *Cymatics* is from the Greek and means *wave*.

We Googled how to make a cymatics board, a device which captures the effects of sound frequencies on a plate or other surface in order to create a display of their unique formations in a liquid or other medium. My oldest son, Jordan, is a musician with an understanding of sound. I asked Jordan and one of our longtime musicians at The Rock of Mobile, Ray Malone, a welder by trade who has a deep understanding of the circle of fifths, to build the cymatics board. So, Jordan and Ray set out to build a cymatics board in our recording studio. We used sand to reveal the patterns that the sound waves produce, but there are many ways to build a cymatic system. It was fun. The shapes created were orderly and amazing. They look like sci-fi creations, but they are reality.

I pondered: what was this for and how would it work as part of the wheel? So many different sensory inputs, such as sound, light, and more, can trigger the brain to function. The human brain is largely made up of gray matter. It houses nearly one hundred billion neurons, which are nerve cells that transmit electrical impulses through electrical and chemical signals. Popular belief states that we only use 10% of our brain's capacity, although science says that belief is a myth. I think it may be true that we use an even smaller percentage of our brain capabilities. This remains a mystery. I believe that when the mind that is of our spirit awakens to its original sounds, then the capacity to properly house the Christ-mind greatly increases. I also believe that the mind is not confined to the brain only. Our entire bodies, when we are in our light and sound form, will be linked to Yahweh's mind. How cool is that?!

We are redeeming the original sounds of what Yahweh has said about us in the scrolls about our minds. As with the complexity of the DNA coding in the second wheel, the third wheel was likewise too complex to attempt to find all of the different designs of the sound that we are to redeem in our mind. So, I circled back to what I was seeing that needed to take place in the transformed second phase that had become a cube.

Basic Shape: The Cube

The cube is one of the five Platonic solids. It is the second one right after the tetrahedron.[13] Yahweh has used the three points of a triangle to build the natural world in which we live. Even though it may not look like it to the natural eye, the cube itself is made up of triangles. The cube has six faces and eight vertices. The new Jerusalem is designed from this geometric shape. All shapes are dimensional, but the cube fits the four corners and the up and the down. What I saw with the cube from the third wheel dealt with the four corners of our minds—it's kind of like the north, south, east and west of our linear world, even though we live on a sphere.[14] As I looked at

---

13 I have broken this down for study in *Come Up Here*. See especially "Platonic Solids," pages 187-190.
14 I know very smart people who claim we are not on a sphere, but I believe their math points to another creation in another dimension.

a cube that was a transformed design from the third wheel, I could see it not only in 3D but in 4D. The fourth dimension changes the time constraints that we are accustomed to here on earth. It's difficult to explain, because it is only discerned by spiritual, dimensional positioning. As you move deeper into Yahweh, by His invitation, you will begin to understand what this all means.

Once I had identified the cube with its four different directions, I noticed doors on each side. There were twelve doors per side. The doors looked like the old disc drive drawers on computer towers. Remember that you would press a button and the door would slide open to insert a disc? It looked just like that and it worked much the same way. Next I saw trumpets at all four corners, with one trumpet per side. The trumpet from the east side made a quick blast: as it did, the top door of the twelve on that side opened. The slot that opened and slid out of the cube looked like a cymatic plane. Its surface was crystalline. The foundations of the New Jerusalem are primarily crystalline. While many natural elements have lost their identity, crystalline structures still hold some of the original characteristics from creation.

The trumpet would make a long blast in order to arrange the signature of the crystals. Once the arrangement was complete, the trumpet would make one quick blast and the drawer holding the plane of crystalline design would return back into the cube. This procedure repeated one by one until all twelve had been arranged.

Once they were all back in their slots, the trumpet, which was alive, waited for a moment, then made a long blast. All came out together as the trumpet sounded and remained so until the long blast stopped. The trumpet again sounded one quick blast, and then they all together returned back into the cube.

This process continued exactly the same way with the trumpet from the north, followed by the trumpet on the south, finishing with the trumpet of the west. Once the process was complete, the trumpets sat in silence for a moment, then all four sounded and all 48 doors opened. As the trumpets all played in unison, they suddenly stopped, and finally all four made a quick blast and all 48 doors returned back into their slots. It was an awesome sight.

Then I saw what happened next. First there was a moment of silence, then a very loud but beautifully amazing blast came from all four trumpets. They continued to sound as the cube itself began to transform and come alive into a tesseract that is alive. The tesseract is the inside-out and outside-in of the throne room of our mind, living and breathing through the trumpets the sounds of *Yud Hey Vav Hey*. Even now writing this, I'm overwhelmed at the greatness. It's suddenly Heaven and earth joined dimensionally in our minds and it produces the 24 faces—not just 4 or 6, but the fourth dimension of 24 faces.

As the throne room of our mind was made alive and the tesseract formed back into the wheel within the wheel, it had found its own original song of the mind of Christ. This sound didn't conflict with the other two wheels of the health wheel and the identity wheel. It harmonized beautifully with them.

The Fourth Wheel

When I began my journey of discovering the wheels within wheels, as I've already mentioned, I thought I would build just the first wheel. I later decided to continue building the second, third and fourth wheels by the invitation of Yahweh and encouragement of my friends. Yahweh said the fourth wheel would be the most difficult. When I finished the third wheel, I was to dedicate my time and keep my focus to finish the fourth wheel with little to no distractions. It took three months during one of the most beautiful summers that I can remember. I love golf, and the summers here in the Deep South of the U.S. are usually too hot to play, especially in the afternoon. Not that summer. There was almost no rain and it wasn't nearly as hot as usual. I kept my focus and stayed inside. Sometimes I wouldn't leave the church property for several days. It's not as bad as it sounds: I live on the back of the property and I slept every night in my bed and didn't miss any meals. But I was dedicated. I didn't speak in my pulpit or play golf for those three months.

As I began to listen by the spirit for this next very mysterious wheel in a wheel, I didn't know what to expect. The first thing I noticed was that the colors of the fourth wheel within a wheel were different. It had musical chords attached in the same order as the others, but numbers were not assigned to these chords. The mind wheel looked similar in that it was a solid color on the outside wheel and a different color on the inside wheel. The first two wheels were colored from the normal pattern of basic light waves that we are accustomed to of red, green and blue. The outside of the fourth wheel is purple. Its inside wheel color is derived from the design of beryllium. Beryllium, the fourth element on the periodic table, is significant in the wheels. Like a glass prism reveals a spectrum, clear, pure beryl, a mineral made up of beryllium aluminum cyclosicate, can reflect, refract, and reveal every color, but light coming through it is primarily teal in color.

Next I saw and heard the three wheels each playing their own sounds three successive times. Afterwards, it was as if they turned to the fourth wheel and in unison played the identity wheel's sound until the fourth wheel began to awaken. It was an awesome new encounter, but I knew it was only new to me in that moment, for the fourth wheel had been as if asleep or on hold. As it was waking up, it began to spin and make the identity sounds with the other three, and I was taken down a mysterious path into the fourth wheel.

The fourth wheel was alive in a different way than the three other wheels. It invited me into its world to build and write what was, and is, and is to come of its purpose. I went deep into its heart and looked through the eyes of this amazing creature. I realized that it desired to tell the story of the John 17 man, the Romans 8 man, the story of us in Him and Him in us. I knew it had to be built and told just the way Yahweh sees it and for us to see it.

The first thing He said to do while drawing out the plans was to create the eye of Yahweh and the eye of man. The eye of Yahweh, in this case, was designed from the pictures of a nebula. The Hubble telescope has produced many beautiful photos of nebula patterns, but the one I chose was the Helix Nebula, for it looks just like an eye. The eye of man was designed similar in pattern to the wheels and their color array.

Yahweh instructed me to go to my swimming pool. There He would show me the wave pattern that we were to draw that extended from the eye of Yahweh and the eye of man. When you are building something for Yahweh's desire, you follow every instruction precisely, no matter how foolish or childlike it may seem. He told me to go at noon when the sun is straight above my head, put my face near the water, and gently blow on the water. "Blow into it until you see the exact pattern that fits Our eyes." "Our eyes?" "Yes." His eye within our eyes and our eyes within His. It was an awesome moment. I remember doing this as a child and being enamored by the patterns. Yahweh uses childish things to build these amazing ancient things that unlock treasures. I asked one of my primary artists, Rachel Miller, to go down to my pool and do the same thing that I did. I asked her to find the pattern that she would see and let us build it from that wavelength. She did it and loved doing it. She said it was like being a kid again. We drew the pattern out as we saw it and as we were instructed. When we completed this step, the next design came forth.

What I saw next was like a sci-fi rendition of a spacecraft. At first I thought I was seeing seed pods, but I knew that it couldn't be because the seed cycle isn't seated here in this dimension. What I saw is best described as discs. The discs were like flying saucers but positioned vertically. There were twelve, and they were large in size. The outsides were ornately designed but not in a recognizable pattern. Each large, silver-gray disc had its own unique design. They were amazing and mysterious. We drew them out the best that we could. The twelve discs were positioned side by side, divided into four groups of three each. I was about to find out why. I was about to find out their purpose, too.

I could tell the discs were suspended and waiting on their activation. Yahweh said to me to turn our eyes upon the discs and watch them awaken. As we did, each disc came alive and began to open up and reveal what was on the inside. One by one they began to unfold. We heard His voice first, for we didn't know we were blind. Now we were hearing and seeing, too. I didn't yet understand the living letters through Eber. I understand it much better now, but one reason it was so special is that we had the voice of Yahweh guiding us.

The Acts and Scenes of Us in Creation

The discs were unfolding the story of us in creation. It was a four-act play with twelve scenes per act. Each disc housed four acts that contributed to the twelve scenes per act. There were a total of 48 scenes for the entire play. The four acts represented the four corners of creation. The twelve scenes represented the government of God in all things. The number 48 is an ancient number. It represents the fullness of all that creation is capable of producing without the glorified sons of Yahweh governing it.

The four acts represented the following:

- **Act One:** The original plan in the garden

- **Act Two:** The fall of man and the curse upon creation

- **Act Three:** The redemptive plan of Yahweh with Yahshua as the Kinsman-Redeemer

- **Act Four:** We who are called by His name becoming the John 17 man

We were individuals in this fourth act, special to Yahweh's heart in our own way, yet we were joined to Him and to each other. It's the play of us in Him and Him in us and us in each other.

When I thought the story couldn't get any better, Yahweh had a surprise finish to the play. Yahweh said to me, "Look and see the finish." As I did, I saw us standing as one witness and then I saw the Godhead of Yahweh, Yahshua, and Ruach Kodesh standing as one witness. He then said this: "You are the 49th witness and we are the 50th witness." I immediately knew it was Jubilee! He was declaring Jubilee: the returning back to the original intent of all He has ever desired. He joins us and we join Him in declaring *50* on earth. Then all of Heaven rejoices and joins their *50* from Heaven to give us our 100-fold return!

I have not been able to record all of the details here, but here is a hint. Each wheel was supported by its own quadrant of constellations which align with the twelve tribes of Israel. The four Gospels were also honored, along with four primary archangels that assist us even to this day. The elements of the earth were represented in the wheels themselves. All creation is groaning for its sound to be heard—and it is being heard.

I asked Oracle Teresa Bowen, who helped in the entirety of the project, to write out of her spirit the story of the fourth wheel. What resulted is amazing! From what she wrote, she published *The Fourth Wheel Story: New Creation Man.*[15] The book includes copies of the original drawings from the four-act play, created by Breanna Veth, Rachel Miller, Teresa Bowen and me. (I don't consider myself an artist but I guess we all

---

15   Mobile, AL: Scrolls of Zebulon, 2017.

can be at times.) I drew my rendition of Eden and of the four rivers. I enjoyed it—but the true artists took it to another level. It was an amazing endeavor that led to a question I had for Yahweh.

I was perplexed because I believed we had properly completed the fourth wheel, but it didn't seem to be the most difficult of the wheels. There was much to it, but it flowed. I thought in my heart that the first wheel was more difficult because everything was new. I felt I needed to enquire of the Lord about this puzzling matter. He simply said to take our drawings of the fourth wheel upstairs, where my son Joshua was working.

Coding Beyond *Yes* and *No*

Joshua, with his team, had been coding the wheels by computer in order for me to see and interact with what the wheels were producing. We had drawn all of the fourth wheel plans and designs out on a ten-foot long piece of butcher-type paper. It was very detailed. In some places of the storied timeline we had several layers of drawings. I entered the room where many computers with multiple elaborate screens were displayed. I love watching geeks work, especially with all of their sci-fi tech gadgets and lava lamps arranged around their work area in random places. They love little unique snacks and will work for days on end with little rest if they find the project they have been assigned challenging. Well, I had no idea that I was about to overload their circuit.

As I walked into their office, I had the rolled up drawings in my hand. Joshua asked, "What is that?" I responded that it was the fourth wheel. I unrolled it, excited to show them our masterpiece. I laid it out on the floor. They began looking it over as I shared its greatness. To my total surprise, they were silent. I knew what we had created was Yahweh's heart and it was truly amazing, so their silence shocked me. I asked them, "What is wrong?"

Joshua said, "Dad, this is so cool, but it would take thousands of programmers years to render it." He explained that some of the interactions of this wheel would require technology that didn't exist yet. I was confused. I rolled my plan up and went back to my office.

I asked Yahweh if He could explain. He responded that I had not yet asked Joshua the right question. He added that He had warned me that the fourth wheel would be the most difficult wheel to accomplish. I sighed and returned back upstairs to the geek cave.

As I re-entered their office, they were already back on their computers, coding graphics for the other wheels. They didn't even look up from their keyboards or screens, I guess fearing another impossible request. Techies, like these amazing young people, immerse themselves in a project in order to deliver nearly impossible results, and I had asked something beyond their ability.

I asked Joshua to give an account of their accomplishments. They had been coding for long days over the course of months. He showed me some of the results. I was so proud. They had coded over 200,000 lines. As they scrolled down their screens, it looked like the movie *The Matrix*. The graphics that the code had produced were awesome: they were interactive. The graphics for much of the first wheel and some of the second wheel were working perfectly and transforming the way I had seen it. Joshua said there were still hundreds of thousands of lines of code left, though, in order to complete just the first wheel.

I asked Joshua *the question*: "What is taking so long?"

He answered that the computer could care less about my graphics—it only understands basically one train of thought, and that is 0s and 1s.

I said in ignorance, "I thought these computers were supposed to be smart."

He replied, "They have great abilities through amazing programs, but all programs come down to the 0s and 1s." The eureka-moment of a lifetime came when he added that the 0s and 1s were like *yes* and *no*.

I stood there totally jolted. "Why?"

Yahweh had given me a short series to teach back in the mid-nineties that not only confused those I tried to teach but confused me. Don't misunderstand me. We learned much from the teaching, but it didn't seem pertinent to what we were doing at the time. The series was titled "Urim and Thummim," which are also known as the *yes* and *no* of Yahweh. Immediately, there in the room with Joshua and his gang, I had a download from Yahweh. Yahweh said to me, "I've only given them (the world) the *yes* and *no*, but I'll give you the rest of the language."

I was awakened to the purpose to much of what we were doing within that instant. I not only saw the revelation of the language, I also saw divine designs and witty inventions that would forever change the world.[16]

---

16 I will cover more about Urim and Thummim and witty inventions in Part 2.

I had a download of a new and much better way of computing. Yahweh said that the time had come and we had entered the dimensions of greatness that would require the sons of Yahweh to begin ruling the earth for righteousness' sake. The Love of Yahweh had abounded and the sons were awakening to their position and place. Yahweh said that all computing and everything concerning computing had been on loan to the sons of the earth from the speaking place, the throne room of Yahweh. He had only given them the *yes* and *no,* for the sons of the earth did not desire communion with Yahweh—they only wanted an answer. Now that the sons of Yahweh were engaging with Yahweh by communing with Him and not on their own terms but His, it gave way to the right to be seated. When Yahweh invited us into our throne rooms, it enabled the doors that had been shut for ages to be opened for Yahweh Himself. Now, Almighty Yahweh, our Elohim, has set Himself to speak to His creation only through us, His family.

That's right—I really do believe that. And yes—you read that correctly. It is no longer appropriate to ask God to fix things, for we speak together as family from our throne rooms. Is He still the authority? Absolutely! Always! He is the only authority, but He rules from within that authority with us and through us. He will rule from this place with His family over all creation forever.

◢ ◢ ◢

These were the first signs to me that Yahweh was revealing new but yet ancient secrets and paths. He was opening up the prison doors for us to be free indeed. Our freedom that was purchased by our Messiah and King, Yahshua, also came with an invitation to be seated with Him.

How glorious is that?!

2

VEILED COMMUNICATIONS

In order to be of the big reveal, I believe it is imperative that the veil cannot remain upon the hearts and minds of those designed to be glorious.

In my years of ministry, I've noticed major pitfalls that hinder people from deeper spiritual experiences. In this brief chapter, I attempt to lay out a simple plan to enable those who are interested in doing so to break through the veil. Beyond the veil lie the paths that lead to the depths of knowing Yahweh's greatness, so I urge you, do not wait any longer to pursue fulfilling this part of your purpose.

The Veil Torn

Let us first look into the amazing story of the veil that was torn in two when Yahshua changed dimensions. We begin with Yahshua on the cross:

> [50] ...*Jesus cried out again with a loud voice, and yielded up His spirit.*

⁵¹ Then, behold, the veil of the temple was torn in two from top to bottom; and the earth quaked, and the rocks were split, ⁵² and the graves were opened; and many bodies of the saints who had fallen asleep were raised; ⁵³ and coming out of the graves after His resurrection, they went into the holy city and appeared to many. (Matt. 27:50–53 NKJV)

The temple veil, it is believed, was 60 feet long by 30 feet wide and 4 inches thick. Its large size required 300 priests to move it. The veil protected man from Yahweh's glory which was present at times within the veil. If someone were to go behind the veil without following the protocol from Heaven, the glory within could kill. The glory of Yahweh is heavy, it is piercing: sin cannot abide near it.

Today, many behave as though there is a veil that remains around Yahweh. But Yahshua, in His love for the Father, gave way for the veil to be torn in two. It is important to note that the veil was rent (as the King James Version states), or torn, from top to bottom. The specific direction of the tearing from top to bottom speaks of Heaven as the initiator. Ever since the veil was torn, there has been an open Heaven ready to accept us and communicate with us. The gift of the grace of God through Yahshua's blood protects us from the heaviness of the glory of God. If it wasn't for this amazing grace, we would be crushed by the glory.

Sin has always been the hindrance against man entering into relationship and communion with Yahweh. The spotless lamb, represented by Yahshua, became the ultimate sacrifice for sin. Yahshua cleared the way for the law to no longer keep the veil over our hearts and keep us out of the presence of Yahweh. Those of us who have accepted Yahshua the Christ as our Lord and Savior have been given the power of the leverage of His blood. The blood of Yahshua was pure and spotless from sin: thus the blood of Yahshua has cleansed us and leveraged us from our sins. Amazing!

Second Corinthians 3:1–18 addresses how we can communicate and be in communion with Yahweh. Consider specifically the following:

> [12] *Therefore, since we have such hope, we use great boldness of speech—* [13] *unlike Moses, who put a veil over his face so that the children of Israel could not look steadily at the end of what was passing away.* [14] *But their minds were blinded. For until this day the same veil remains unlifted in the reading of the Old Testament, because the veil is taken away in Christ.* [15] *But even to this day, when Moses is read, a veil lies on their heart.* [16] *Nevertheless when one turns to the Lord, the veil is taken away.* [17] *Now the Lord is the Spirit; and where the Spirit of the Lord is, there is liberty.* [18] *But we all, with unveiled face, beholding as in a mirror the glory of the Lord, are being transformed into the same image from glory to glory, just as by the Spirit of the Lord.* (2 Cor. 3:12–18 NKJV)

If Yahweh has removed the veil separating Himself from us, then why do we have such a difficult time believing we can communicate with Him? We have become His temple (1 Cor. 3:16; 1 Cor. 6:19) where there is no veil. Maybe the veil that hinders communication today isn't His veil. Perhaps those who seem unable to communicate have placed a veil upon their own hearts.

If this is the case, let us look at the probable causes for the phenomenon. What is the phenomenon? Think about it: to have the Almighty Holy One Yahweh tear the veil in two, reveal who He is, desire communion with a people who have been given rights to join in communication—and they refuse to believe it? That's more of an enigmatic mystery.

I believe this serious problem comes from slavery of the flesh and religion. But remember, it is recorded in John 8:36 that Yahshua said, *"If the Son therefore shall make you free, ye shall be free indeed"* (KJV). In my previous book, *Come Up Here*, I break down the four slave systems that have kept us from freedom.[17] If Yahshua is your Lord, then you are free, and if you are free, then act like it. How do you do that? Disassociate from the slave systems. Freedom is available for us and an amazing relationship awaits.

If He Says It's Finished...

Let me tell a story here that I believe will help us understand how we can be fooled by our surroundings when by the words of Yahweh things are already settled.

My grandmother was a twin. She and her twin also had another sister, and they lived their entire lives, each into their eighties and nineties, next door to each other. All three loved God. They were women of prayer. The entire neighborhood knew when they were praying. My grandmother had reached her eighties and was facing health issues. She needed surgery

17 See Aaron Smith, "The Four Slave Systems," pp. 170-184, in *Come Up Here: The Place of Our Original Intent* (Mobile, AL: Scrolls of Zebulon, 2016).

and was greatly dreading it. I never heard her complain about much in life, but she had never before had health problems and this surgery had her worried. She repeatedly said how much she couldn't wait until it was over. At the time, you would be hospitalized for nearly any surgical procedure. While she was in the hospital awaiting surgery, we visited with her. She quietly prayed to and praised God.

She finally had the surgery and remained under anesthesia for a while. Afterwards, she was brought back to her room for recovery. When she woke up, all the family visiting were sitting there with her.

She said, "I am dreading this surgery so much, and I will be so glad when it is over."

We all looked at each other and smiled. We told her the surgery was over.

The most confused look came over her face. She asked with curious optimism, "What did you say?"

We repeated, "It is already done."

My mother had to prove it to her by showing her. Having now seen the bandaged area, my grandmother still had a puzzled look on her face. She asked, "How did that happen?" Then she began to praise God so loudly people thought she had lost her mind, but we were laughing and excited for her.

I've thought of this episode many times. Often, Yahweh has already taken care of something I am dreading. Our example of communicating with our Father and believing in faith should be this: if He said it is finished, then it is finished. When we stay in communion with Him, our emotions will not be in vain. Instead, we will be aligned with His glory.

The Thinking Chair

Recently, I was on my back porch rocking in my favorite chair. It's my thinking chair. Sometimes it has other names like *whining chair*, or *complaining chair*, but at times it is also my *thankful chair*.

It is almost like a schizophrenic chair, if you will. *Schizophrenia* is defined as "a long-term mental disorder of a type involving a breakdown in the relation between thought, emotion, and behavior, leading to faulty perception, inappropriate actions and feelings, withdrawal from reality [*caution: note that reality of the spirit is more real than that of the natural—A.S.*] and personal relationships into fantasy and delusion, and a sense of mental fragmentation".[18] Don't miss my inserted note in the definition: the spiritual is more real than the natural. Associate with that and reverse the thinking. In that chair, there were times I would praise God, and then immediately feel totally defeated and almost helpless. My mood depended on decisions I was facing and how serious the consequences could be.

You see, the tech company that I started came out of my studies from Ezekiel chapters 1 and 10 and Revelation chapter 4. We are pioneering a unique new encryption technology in a field that has been virtually untouched. Our technology is primarily in the nano-dimension—we basically guide photons. Pioneering a new technology can be a slow-go and the process can be pressure-packed. It has been an amazing ride that has produced incredible patents, and I love it. But, I will love it more when funds are returning to us instead of

---

18 "Schizophrenia." Oxford Living Dictionaries: English. Accessed June 26, 2018. https://en.oxforddictionaries.com/definition/schizophrenia.

only going out, if you know what I mean. I see the project as a great opportunity for many to get out of debt and poverty. I want to see a return for my business partners who have invested big funds. I want it for all of us.

Several of my friends, along with many family members, have believed with me in the establishment of the company and have given me funds to support it. I have three primary investors and business partners, but the rest of the funding has come through gifts given out of love and belief. When our project runs out of funds—which has been often due to the expenses of the high tech field we are in—I deal emotionally and spiritually with whatever is happening.

In pressure-filled moments, we sometimes get everyone's advice but Yahweh's. We call this counsel-seeking and advice-gathering "being responsible," and I'm sure there is a place for it, but when you don't have the answers, I advise you: don't make the mistake of continually asking people their opinions. Those giving advice may care for you and your project, but Yahweh is jealous that we ask Him first out of our relationship and communion with Him. I know He knows the answer to every problem, but I'm not sure I know yet how to hear Him clearly under extreme pressure. That has been an issue for me, and hearing Him clearly is something I am pursuing.

So, one day not long ago I was seated in my chair on my back porch. That day was an "Oh, God!" day—and not an "Oh, God" day as in crying out to Him, if you understand my expression. My cry was, "Oh, God, what am I going to do?" Imminent disaster loomed for the company and all we'd worked for. I finally swapped my chair from a chair of giving in to fear into one of giving my attention to Yahweh.

I asked Him, "What am I to do?" I told Him I was as convinced as ever that He had given the company to me, and I still believed it was designed to greatly succeed.

Suddenly, Yahweh asked me a question. Questions from Yahweh can be scary, for they usually have to do with something I've wavered on. Sometimes His questions are truly inquisitive, and lead me to a mystery I'm meant to search out, but other times the questions are meant to challenge my confusion and disbelief. (Regardless, I love His questions and always invite them for they are an important part of communication in a healthy relationship.)

Yahweh plainly asked me if I believed Psalm 24. My immediate response was, "Absolutely! Of course I do, with all of my heart."

His swift response to me was, "THEN ACT LIKE IT!"

Was He yelling? Yes, but in a firm and loving way. You should know what I mean. It was like, "Come on—what are you doing? Get with it!"

Yahweh spoke to me from the entire chapter of Psalms 24, but He strictly emphasized verses 7–10.

> *⁷ Lift up your heads, O you gates!*
> *And be lifted up, you everlasting doors!*
> *And the King of glory shall come in.*
>
> *⁸ Who is this King of glory?*
> *The Lord strong and mighty,*
> *The Lord mighty in battle.*
>
> *⁹ Lift up your heads, O you gates!*
> *Lift up, you everlasting doors!*
> *And the King of glory shall come in.*

¹⁰ Who is this King of glory?
The Lord of hosts,
He is the King of glory. Selah (NKJV)

He said, "I FIGHT THIS BATTLE FOR YOU!" He went on to tell me to make my seat a mercy seat. The mercy was mercy to me first, and then to everything around me that wasn't measuring up. He said that once I could maintain this seat of mercy, then the seat would become and remain the seat of peace. How great is that?!

Yahweh battled greatly for me and the way He took care of my problem was beyond my comprehension. The solution He provided had no sorrow, no regrets that came with it. It came within two weeks of my recognizing the seat of mercy and truly acknowledging that Yahweh fights for me. Proverbs 10:22 explains, *"The blessing of the Lord, it maketh rich, and he addeth no sorrow with it"* (KJV). I'll receive that way of operation while never forgetting Psalm 24.

Avoiding Pitfalls

At the beginning of the chapter I mentioned pitfalls which can hinder you from deep, spiritual experiences with Yahweh. But you shouldn't be afraid of those experiences, for a deeper walk will enable you to know His voice clearly. Think of the following passage from John. After Yahshua says, *"Father, glorify your name,"* a voice from Heaven makes the announcement:

²⁸ "I have both glorified it and will glorify it again."
²⁹ Therefore the people who stood by and heard it said that it had thundered. Others said, "An angel has spoken to Him." (John 12:28–29 NKJV)

Would you have heard thunder? Would you have heard an angel? Would you have heard His voice? Would you know the difference?

You should be able to notice what is spiritual by nature and not be confused about what is and what is not. The experience of knowing Him from within the veil will rework your grid. As it becomes reality for you, you will begin to realize the power of everlasting life.

Let us look at some pitfalls common to those seeking more. Habakkuk 2:1 states, *"I will stand upon my watch, and set me upon the tower, and will watch to see what he will say unto me, and what I shall answer when I am reproved"* (KJV).

You cannot be afraid to be called flaky or weird. Those who try to measure up to what man expects and accepts never see the treasures of the spirit world of Yahweh. Make yourself wide open to the depths of Yahweh's greatness, for the depths provide never ending paths to His goodness and His amazing treasures. When the next experience comes—and it will, if you make yourself available—then acknowledge it by saying so, or even by giving something as simple as a nod. Don't talk yourself out of what just happened. If you are determined to do this, you will break the barrier, or maybe better said, you will go through the veil. When you do this, your faith has aligned to the dimensions opened up to you.

Take a look at the following table and consider: which of the pitfalls have you faced or do you face? Have you applied solutions to deal with them?

Pitfalls That Hinder the Believer
from Spiritual Experiences

Pitfall	Solution
Not believing you can hear and see	If you have believed enough to know you are saved and being born again, then **believe you can see and hear**. It is just that simple.
Not recognizing the dimensions of the spirit world of Yahweh that require faith	People see things by the spirit, but they reason away what they see and hear due to the effects of slavery. **Receive the freedom that Yahshua has purchased** and never walk in slavery again.[19]
Not being able to engage spiritual experiences when they attempt to engage with you	Spiritual experiences come when you are not expecting them. The key is to **take the time to stop and acknowledge spiritual experiences**, and then not reason the experiences away.

It is impossible to be of the big reveal without knowing how to acknowledge and engage the dimensions of Yahweh and His amazing creation. It is the place that we fit perfectly within, and it fits perfectly within us.

All you have to do is believe.

---

19 See Aaron Smith, "The Four Slave Systems," pp. 170-184 from *Come Up Here: The Place of Our Original Intent* (Mobile, AL: Scrolls of Zebulon, 2016) and Romans 8.

3

THE MYSTERY OF KING CYRUS
AND THE TWO LEAVED GATES

L et's begin this chapter by reading about King Cyrus, Yahweh's anointed. It is of utmost importance to engage with the revelation of the following scripture. If you have read it a hundred times, please read it again, but this time, engage with the Seven Spirits of the Lord as you read.

> *¹ Thus saith the Lord to his anointed, to Cyrus, whose right hand I have holden, to subdue nations before him; and I will loose the loins of kings, to open before him the two leaved gates; and the gates shall not be shut;*
>
> *² I will go before thee, and make the crooked places straight: I will break in pieces the gates of brass, and cut in sunder the bars of iron:*
>
> *³ And I will give thee the treasures of darkness, and hidden riches of secret places, that thou mayest know*

that I, the Lord, which call thee by thy name, am the
God of Israel.

⁴ For Jacob my servant's sake, and Israel mine elect, I
have even called thee by thy name: I have surnamed
thee, though thou hast not known me.

⁵ I am the Lord, and there is none else, there is no God
beside me: I girded thee, though thou hast not known
me:

⁶ That they may know from the rising of the sun,
and from the west, that there is none beside me. I am
the Lord, and there is none else.

⁷ I form the light, and create darkness: I make peace, and
create evil: I the Lord do all these things.

⁸ Drop down, ye heavens, from above, and let the skies
pour down righteousness: let the earth open, and let
them bring forth salvation, and let righteousness spring
up together; I the Lord have created it. (Isa. 45:1–8).

Many points in this scripture are pertinent for today, but
one thing stands out as relevant for now: the two leaved gates.
Before I give my view of who Cyrus is, I must first identify
that I agree with many that King Cyrus was a physical type
and shadow of what we can expect today. He delivered Israel
from Babylon. Today, we live in Babylonian captivity, knowing
that deliverance is near. Indeed, we actively look for who it is
that will open the double leaf gates.

Many have tried to identify Cyrus in their own era, but
their attempts to proclaim particular men to be the modern-
day Cyrus never seem to pan out. My interpretation may have

the same end, but I don't think it will (as I'm sure all the others must have thought). I have a new twist. Here's a question to start: If Cyrus is here now or has already done his thing, where is he?

We may agree that identifying Cyrus is important, but is the place important? Absolutely! The place I speak from is the United States.

Yahweh hates Babylon. Let us be very clear with that. He has declared the result of man's arrogance and self-reliance to be confusion.[20] Babylon is driven by pride. Pride is upheld by the financial status one desires to achieve. In short, Babylon is about money and the love of it. In the Babylonian world, money speaks and can get you into or out of most any place, position, or situation. Revelation chapter 18 addresses the ultimate demise that awaits Babylon. *"Babylon the great is fallen, is fallen,"* John wrote after he prophetically saw and revealed the future (Rev. 18:2). Babylon is a system of man's desires and ways of managing his financial world and everything in it, and it cannot stand.

The Book of Isaiah reveals that King Cyrus defeated the historic Babylon. Today, Cyrus has already shown up, beginning when the ages began their change in 2007–2008 and finally changed in August of 2009.[21] I believe Cyrus the Great has not shown up as one person, or even a person at all, but a Word, a heart, a spirit.

Before we get into the two leaved gates, let's look into a few questions. First, the question: who is Cyrus? From scripture we know Yahweh holds his right hand, that he is a

---

20 Review the story of the Tower of Babel in Genesis 11, especially verses 6–7.
21 I detail the subject of the ages in my previous book, *Come Up Here.*

deliverer, and the double gate opener (Isa. 45:1). Cyrus is the answer to the cry for change and greatness. I do not believe he is just one person, but that he represents many of our time now who cry out for their opportunity. Cyrus was not of the house of Israel and did not know Yahweh (vv.3–5), but he became Yahweh's chosen deliverer. Yahweh marked him as the deliverer and gave him everything needed to complete the job. We can't forget that when Yahweh says something is over, it is over. Yahweh made a way to deliver Israel from the captivity of Babylon through King Cyrus.

Where is the place? It is anywhere the system is engaged and working. I must be clear, though: I see the United States of America as the epitome of the Babylonian system. Likewise, Europe fits, as do most of the world's financial powerhouses. However, Singapore, as a financial powerhouse, is being set up as a place that Yahweh desires to use as a pivotal point of leverage against Babylon's strength. Some may surmise that with this kind of thinking, I must be against capitalism and lean toward socialism. My response? No way!

Capitalism defined is:

> an economic system characterized by private or corporate ownership of capital goods, by investments that are determined by private decision, and by prices, production, and the distribution of goods that are determined mainly by competition in a free market.[22]

---

22 "Capitalism." Merriam-Webster. Accessed December 29, 2017. https://www.merriam-webster.com/dictionary/capitalism.

Socialism defined is:

1: any of various economic and political theories advocating collective or governmental ownership and administration of the means of production and distribution of goods

2 a: a system of society or group living in which there is no private property

b: a system or condition of society in which the means of production are owned and controlled by the state.[23]

I believe in the ownership that capitalism encourages. However, I know that Yahweh is the owner of all things. Consider this scripture in which Yahshua describes the ownership process: *"All things that the Father hath are mine: therefore said I, that he shall take of mine, and shall shew it unto you"* (John 16:15). All that I have really belongs to Yahweh. I don't own anything: yet through Him, I own it all.

I love being an American. I'm moved by the playing of our national anthem, "The Star-Spangled Banner." When I travel abroad, I am always happy to know that I've reentered U.S. airspace. Why? It's home. I don't love the greed that I see driving my homeland. Perhaps it is time for us all to face up to the truth about our homelands, wherever they may be—to face up to the fact that they all are driven in some way by the Babylonian ways of man. Babylon is in most everything— even in our churches. Yahweh and His Kingdom is the only everlasting place, or should I say, home.

---

23 "Socialism." Merriam-Webster. Accessed December 29, 2017. https://www.merriam -webster.com/dictionary/socialism.

Now to my point. What and who are the two leaved gates? The gates represent the way to exit the control of the Babylonian system and the way to enter Yahweh's system of government. Former President Barack Obama and President Donald Trump are the two leaved gates. President Obama represents a cry for change, a cry to exit the slavery of the old system—the system of Babylon. He was elected primarily by minorities who felt like they didn't count.[24] President Trump represents a cry for greatness. He was elected primarily by the Electoral college vote, the working class who felt overlooked.[25] While President Trump represents a cry for greatness, it is a greatness that only the Kingdom of Yahweh can ultimately offer.

A Nation's Cry for Change; A Nation's Cry for Greatness

President Obama's cry was for change. What a statement that an African American who not long ago had no rights now became leader of the free world was amazing and historic to say the least. He was inaugurated January 20, 2009 as the 44th United States President, having garnered 95% of the African American vote.[26] Personally, I didn't support his candidacy due to his liberal stance. I questioned how any believer of any race could overlook Obama's morally wrong views. They seemed only to focus on his racial background as an African American with a chance to become president. Later, I would come to ponder how deep the wounds of racism and prejudice must be that those of us who are not African American couldn't

24 See, for example, Tom Rosentiel. "Inside Obama's Sweeping Victory." Pew Research Center. https://www.pewresearch.org/2008/11/05/inside-obamas-sweeping-victory/.
25 Drew DeSilver. "Why Electoral College Wins Are Bigger than Popular Vote Ones." Pew Research Center. December 20, 2016. https://www.pewresearch.org/fact-tank/2016/12/20/why-electoral-college-landslides-are-easier-to-win-than-popular-vote-ones/.
26 Rosentiel, *op. cit.*, footnote 24

possibly understand. I wanted to vote for him because of his charisma and his gentle, yet strong oratory skills that could greatly move his audience. What a statement that an African American man, who not long ago had no rights in our country, now could realistically become leader of the free world. That moment in time was amazing and historic to say the least. In spite of that, I couldn't bring myself to vote for him because of his support for wickedness and perversion. He fed an entitlement mentality of being owed something that didn't help the change he desired to facilitate.

Eventually that mentality created the opportunity for Donald Trump to become President in 2016 via a protest vote. His election may have been less a vote for Trump than it was a vote against the weak status quo that Obama had introduced. Trump's motto was "Make America Great Again." The election of President Trump was astounding. Many who voted for him would never have supported such a dividing and controversial figure in the past.

President Obama represented a judgment of the appearance of freedom and change for justice, but he offered at best a mingled view and sound. Barack Obama states he is a Christian, but it seemed he supported the Muslim view at times more than that of Christianity. However, I was greatly moved when he sang "Amazing Grace" at the funeral of the African American pastor slain by a white racist young man in South Carolina. Obama sang from his heart. I will never forget that. It was not rehearsed, but it was also obviously not his first time to sing it: the emotion was real.

Obama appeared to be against Israel and that never is a good thing since Israel is the measuring rod of most all of Yahweh's judgments.

Many viewed Obama as important, as an African American man who would be symbolically delivered from the slave system to become the leader of the free world. Yet this view oversimplifies Obama's cultural background. He was anything but that. His background is multiracial. His mother was white and his father from Kenya; both were highly educated. There was no slavery background from either side. He grew up in Hawaii, Washington state, and Indonesia, and attended college preparatory school. His color, but not his personal history, represent what a slave in America looked like. During and subsequent to his election, a common question was whether he could relate to the plight that black America has faced? I'm sure he could, due to his multiracial background, at least better than whites.

Donald Trump doesn't fully represent those who voted for him either. Gung-ho voters developed blindspots to certain aspects of his character. He is very rich and out of touch with the economic reality of working-class Americans. Yet his message for greatness was embraced by patriotic, conservative voters. He is in many ways the opposite of Barrack Obama. Obama leaned toward socialist policies, a strength killer of capitalism. Trump is an unabashed capitalist.

Trump is not a politician, shares none of Obama's conciliatory oratorical skill, and has broken most political rules. He seems to thrive on controversy and a fight. He is continually on the attack to reveal politicians' façades: he will tweet about anything and anyone at any time. As of this writing, he has seemed to escape every potential disaster and downfall. He is an enigma to those who thought they had everything in government figured out.

Yet God, very clearly to me, placed both Obama and Trump in the office of the President of the United States. Neither one fixed or will be able to fix this corrupt system. Still, both men were ordained to make a way for the gates to be opened wide in order to bring our release from Babylonian slavery. All things are being judged—or maybe they have already been judged.

From a logical standpoint, President Trump was even less likely to be elected than Obama. By logic and nature, his chances were slim to none. Almost everyone thought it was a joke on his part to even run. It seemed to be a stunt to bring attention to some new TV program or business venture he had planned. The day he was elected shocked everyone who would admit it, and I believe it even shocked him. Trump is breaking the hidden chains that privately and somewhat quietly bind the "regular folks" from making it and having a chance. Actually, it is a similar story to what many thought Obama would bring—a place for a better opportunity to succeed. He instead opened his side of the door that will lead out of Babylon.

It is odd to me that conservative Christians (from the same philosophy and viewpoints with which I was raised) unapologetically cheer on a man who is an example of so many things they have stood against. I could give a list of offenses against Christian morals that Trump has committed, but most everyone knows. In the scheme of philosophies and religions in the world I would consider myself a Christian, but it is the blood of Yahshua that bought my salvation to become part of His family, not a religion. So, if you wondering where I stand, here it is: I'm family, a son, and royalty, as all who believe Romans 8 should believe and think.

I believe through his position as president, God is using Trump to bring judgment against the weakness of the religious church. The measuring rod of judgment that the church has used to measure others now measures them. President Trump is destroying the political system and weakening the strength of the media. The media do not know how to handle him, and I cheer this on. Trump will, in time, swing the other door to freedom from Babylon into the glory of what Yahweh's plan has been all along. One of the evidences of King Cyrus in President Trump is his return of the United States' recognition that Jerusalem belongs to Israel. That is a big deal and a direct analogy.

As Americans, we are taught the Pledge of Allegiance: "I pledge allegiance to the Flag of the United States of America, and to the Republic for which it stands, one Nation under God, indivisible, with liberty and justice for all." Awesome! The big problem is that we are not living up to that standard. I wonder: have we ever?

The United States has been a great place for safety and celebration of freedoms and prosperity, but Yahweh is offended at her for turning her back on Israel. I'm thankful that she is becoming Israel's protector once again for this will extend her legitimacy.

A Visit to the Capital Stairs

At about the time of the Great Exchange in 2008, I visited a friend, an American football celebrity and an outspoken believer of God, who lived just outside of Washington, D.C. He had been the MVP of the NFL in 2005 and aspired to continue his playing career even though he was older than most professional football players. He never played again, but remains a great leader. I stayed in his home, and he and his wife were gracious hosts. They have beautiful, well-behaved children who exemplify their great parenting.

I asked him one day if we could go and walk up the steps of the nation's capital. Two of his young daughters went with us. At the time, he was mentoring a young man, Jacob, a law student at Georgetown University. We stopped by Georgetown to pick him up on our way to the Capital. It was a beautiful April spring day. Washington itself is a beautiful city, but especially in the spring. We parked near the Capital and first toured the botanical gardens just off the west entrance. We then began our walk to the steps that lead up to where presidential inaugurations are held.

As we ascended the many steps, I began to hear a hissing sound and then a sound of many waters. For a reason I didn't understand, I became overwhelmed with emotion. I made sure the guys didn't see me until I noticed they were emotional, too. At first, no one said a word—nor could we.

We ascended as far up the steps as security would allow us. Then we stopped and turned to look from the steps. I asked the guys if they could hear what I was hearing.

Still affected by the deep emotion we were experiencing, they said, "Yes."

I asked, "What is it?"

Suddenly it was revealed to us. We realized it was the sound of prayers going up to Heaven. The cry was "Mercy, have mercy."

I asked Yahweh who was making the sound. He said it was the cries of the saints from our nation and around the world calling out for mercy. I cautiously asked him what his response would be. He said, "I will have mercy on her."

      *   *   *

Until this day, He still has. When the Kingdom of God is fully established on earth as it is in Heaven, then *"the earth shall be filled with the knowledge of the glory of the Lord, as the waters cover the sea"* (Hab. 2:14).

I encourage us all to rid ourselves from the attempted influences of lingering voices of the past. These voices are nothing but echoes at best and attempt to hold us to the slavery of curses. Never allow the curses of poverty, prejudice, pride and unforgiveness to speak again. All of these sounds can be canceled out with the sounds of Heaven Yahweh declares over you and me. Make a joyful sound unto the Lord! First Peter 2:9 says, *"But you are a chosen race who serve as Priests for The Kingdom, a holy people, a redeemed assembly; you should proclaim the praises of him who called you from darkness into his excellent light."*[27]

We who are of the family of God are one Holy race of people! We aren't divided by our differences for our unique qualities make us into the complete and celebrated family of Yahweh.

---

27 The Original Aramaic New Testament in Plain English – with Psalms and Proverbs. Copyright © 2007; 8th edition Copyright © 2013. All rights reserved. Used by Permission.

It is imperative in order for us to be of the big reveal and to complete the desire of Yahweh in destroying Babylon, we must be a whole family and one family. We are never to be divided into races or any other dividing factor. We are one.

Let us finish this chapter with another declaration.

Yahweh this day we engage our scrolls that describe our lives that have been washed in the blood of Yahshua. Where there have been deep wounds of prejudice try to identify us, we ask once and forever to rid ourselves of this horrible identity and indictment that not only is against us but from us. These scrolls do not identify with prejudice, wounds or hidden hurts. We are free, now and forever! By the help of the Holy Ghost we will never bring this up in our memory again. We are now seated in our position and place of glory with Christ and nothing shall separate us from this glorious place. All of this be done by our will in which we are assisted by the Holy Ghost and in the name of our Savior, Yahshua. Amen!

4

A GENUINE APOCALYPSE

Yahweh has a desired purpose and outcome for you and me. With that thought in mind, I hope you will carefully and thoroughly read the following scriptures. First, read Isaiah 40:5–10, which begins with a declaration:

> *5 And the glory of the LORD shall be revealed, and all flesh shall see it together: for the mouth of the LORD hath spoken it.*
>
> *6 The voice said, Cry. And he said, What shall I cry? All flesh is grass, and all the goodliness thereof is as the flower of the field:*
>
> *7 The grass withereth, the flower fadeth: because the spirit of the LORD bloweth upon it: surely the people is grass.*
>
> *8 The grass withereth, the flower fadeth: but the word of our God shall stand for ever.*

⁹ O Zion, that bringest good tidings, get thee up into the high mountain; O Jerusalem, that bringest good tidings, lift up thy voice with strength; lift it up, be not afraid; say unto the cities of Judah, Behold your God!

¹⁰ Behold, the Lord God will come with strong hand, and his arm shall rule for him: behold, his reward is with him, and his work before him.

Next consider Romans 8:18–23, which begins "For I reckon the sufferings of this present time are not worthy to be compared with the glory which shall be revealed in us," and it finishes by addressing the redemption of our body.

¹⁸ For I reckon that the sufferings of this present time are not worthy to be compared with the glory which shall be revealed in us.

¹⁹ For the earnest expectation of the creature waiteth for the manifestation of the sons of God.

²⁰ For the creature was made subject to vanity, not willingly, but by reason of him who hath subjected the same in hope,

²¹ Because the creature itself also shall be delivered from the bondage of corruption into the glorious liberty of the children of God.

²² For we know that the whole creation groaneth and travaileth in pain together until now.

²³ And not only they, but ourselves also, which have the firstfruits of the Spirit, even we ourselves groan

*within ourselves, waiting for the adoption, to wit, the
redemption of our body.*

We get a glimpse through these scriptures of Yahweh's
ultimate outcome and purpose: glory. Now, the questions
begin. What is that glory? How do we uncover it? How can it
be revealed in us? Let's dive in to these mysteries.

The Apocalypse and the Hope of Glory

The word *apocalypse* exudes pending disaster. Definitions
of the word vary widely and include everything from a
cataclysmic destruction from the cosmic heavens, to an
uncovering, to a disclosure of knowledge or revelation. The
Book of Revelation is a literal apocalypse. It begins boldly in
verse one, *"The revelation of Jesus Christ which God gave…"* The
second word, *revelation*, is the Greek word *apokalypsis,* defined
as "a disclosure:--appearing, coming, lighten, manifestation, be
revealed, revelation" (Strong's G602). It can also be defined as
a "vision of Heavenly secrets that can make sense of earthly
realities."[28]

I believe most of the definitions are correct in their varied
contexts. However, I desire to focus my definition from where
I'm dimensionally seated, which I take from Colossians 1:27—
*"To whom God would make known what is the riches of the glory
of this mystery among the Gentiles; which is Christ in you the hope
of glory."*

Christ in you, the hope of glory, is not "Jesus in you and
the hope of going to Heaven." Rather, Christ in you and me
is glory's hope. In order for the glory of God to be made

---

28 Bart D. Ehrman, *How Jesus Became God: The Exaltation of a Jewish Preacher from Galilee,*
HarperOne, 2014, p. 59.

manifest in us, we must engage the revealing of Christ in us first. Yes: the first revealing or apocalypse should be to us who are called by His name.

Who is Christ?

I ask us all a question that may seem to be rhetorical, but let me make a point. Who, or even what, is Christ? The seemingly obvious answer is that Christ is Yahshua (His Hebrew name) or Jesus (the more popular and well-known name by man). He is the Christ, but why is He called *the Christ*? Christ is not Jesus's surname. The greatness of knowing the revelation of this is of grave importance.

Consider Matthew 16:13–19.

> [13] *When Jesus came into the region of Caesarea Philippi, He asked His disciples, saying, "Who do men say that I, the Son of Man, am?"*
>
> [14] *So they said, "Some say John the Baptist, some Elijah, and others Jeremiah or one of the prophets."*
>
> [15] *He said to them, "But who do you say that I am?"*
>
> [16] *Simon Peter answered and said, "You are the Christ, the Son of the living God."*
>
> [17] *Jesus answered and said to him, "Blessed are you, Simon Bar-Jonah, for flesh and blood has not revealed this to you, but My Father who is in heaven. [18] And I also say to you that you are Peter, and on this rock I will build My church, and the gates of Hades shall not prevail against it. [19] And I will give you the keys of the kingdom of heaven, and whatever you bind on earth*

*will be bound in heaven, and whatever you loose on
earth will be loosed in heaven.*" (NKJV)

When Simon Bar-Jonah responded out of his spirit
proclaiming, *"You are the Christ, the Son of the living God,"* it
moved Yahshua to rename him. Simon Bar-Jonah's new name
was Peter (*Petros*, or Rock), which stood not only for strength
and foundation, but also revealed all that Christ was to be in
him. Peter didn't engage with this revelation until he was filled
with the Holy Ghost after the death, burial and resurrection
of the Christ, Yahshua, Jesus.

So, what does *Christ* mean? It means *the anointed one.*[29]
Anointing is associated with oil, and oil represents Ruach
Kodesh, the Holy Spirit. Oils were used to fuel the fire in
the candle sticks. The fire represented not only the fire of the
Holy Ghost, but a realization of the Word of God.

The Effects of Christ's Revealing

When Christ is revealed to us and through us, then many
things begin to come to pass. It's as if the light is turned on
to the immense reality that we *"can do all things"* (Phil. 4:13).
The first reality is that we are truly of His family: we are of
Yahshua's bloodline and we have perfected DNA that He
redeemed for us.

Perfected DNA? Yes! With perfected DNA, we have
eternal life and everlasting life. The difference is that one is
spiritual, and one is natural. But, if they are interchangeable,
and since they work together, then they both are spiritually
and naturally discerned. Discernment is key to being able

---

29 Romans 8:2 & 29, 1 Corinthians 15:45

to engage with such an amazing truth. Discernment occurs when the light comes on in an *"A-ha!"* moment.

The question now for many is why isn't it easy to receive this great revelation? Yet it can be easy when Christ is seated in you. Christ in us is the anointing oil of the Holy Ghost of God creating the fire of God in us to reveal. Simple, huh? I believe it is supposed to be, but it is fundamentally a heart condition. If we seek Him with all of our heart, then we get it. I believe it is really meant to be that simple. There is a necessary walking out of the process, but as we stay with the revelation in honor, our walk goes deeper into Him and all that is His.

The Eternal and the Everlasting

The words *eternal*[30] and *everlasting*[31] carry what on the surface may seem to be simple definitions, but in their depths are mind-boggling.

- Eternal: lasting or existing forever; without end or beginning

- Everlasting: lasting forever

Both definitions sound similar, and indeed they are. But, they have some differences. We find the words in Deuteronomy 33:27, which states: *"The eternal God is thy refuge, and underneath are the everlasting arms…"*

The Hebrew קֶדֶם, translated *eternal* in Deuteronomy 33:27, is made up of the Hebrew letters Quph, Dalet, and Mem, transliterated in English as *qedem*. The word is defined in Strong's as "the front, of place (absolutely, the fore part,

---

30   Deut. 33:27, *Strongs* H6923
31   Deut. 33:7, *Strongs* H5769

relatively the East) or time (antiquity); often used adverbially (before, anciently, eastward)" (H6923). By Eber's definition from the Hebrew letters which make up *qedem*, the word *eternal* refers to

> a mystery from the east to a day that never finishes, although it may end, and the open door of Heaven inviting us to the depths of provision to obtain eternal status.

So, eternity is not only future time, but the past and the present as well.

In verse 27 of Deuteronomy, the word *everlasting* is from the Hebrew עוֹלָם or *'owlam*, made up of the letters Ayin, Vav, Lamed, Mem. Strong's defines the word as meaning "properly, concealed, i.e. the vanishing point; generally, time out of mind (past or future), i.e. [...] always(-s), ancient (time), any more, continuance, [...] lasting, perpetual" (H5769). Eber defines *'owlam* as

> the place that reminds us of the hidden spiraling path that keeps us connected to the breath of life while guiding us into the depths of the forever-abode of our eternal, everlasting being.

Everlasting also describes how long something can last, stay, or hold together, live, exist.

Hebrews 7:1–3 describes a state of being where Melchizedek has "neither beginning of days nor end of life."

> *¹ For this Melchizedek, king of Salem, priest of the Most High God, who met Abraham returning from the slaughter of the kings and blessed him, ² to whom also Abraham gave a tenth part of all, first being translated*

"king of righteousness," and then also king of Salem, meaning "king of peace," [3] *without father, without mother, without genealogy, having neither beginning of days nor end of life, but made like the Son of God, remains a priest continually.* (NKJV)

I believe this dimension is now available for us.

The mind of Christ fully embraces this concept of never ending. The mind that is still encumbered by life's normal cycles and patterns has a very difficult time with such thinking. We see these cycles and patterns all around us. The expected life cycle begins at conception. Then, after birth, it is followed by an expected and accepted life span. Finally: death. It's the pattern of the seed.

I've always loved the power and amazing abilities of a seed, but when Yahweh invited me to come Up Here, I saw another reality. Those amazing seeds have a life cycle. Genesis 8:22 is a law: *"While the earth remaineth, seedtime and harvest, and cold and heat, and summer and winter, and day and night shall not cease."* There are two primary points to emphasize in this case.

First is the word *remain* (*remaineth*, from the King James Version). Naturally, it means *to exist.* I agree—but my question is, to remain in what state? A state of being cursed or blessed? I believe the earth is still under the curse of the law. As long as it is under this law, then Genesis 8:22 is in effect. But Romans 8:16–22 has been waiting to declare, "NOW!"

[16] The Spirit itself beareth witness with our spirit, that we are the children of God: [17] And if children, then heirs; heirs of God, and joint-heirs with Christ; if so be that we suffer with him, that we may be also glorified

together. ¹⁸ For I reckon that the sufferings of this present time are not worthy to be compared with the glory which shall be revealed in us. ¹⁹ For the earnest expectation of the creature waiteth for the manifestation of the sons of God. ²⁰ For the creature was made subject to vanity, not willingly, but by reason of him who hath subjected the same in hope, ²¹ Because the creature itself also shall be delivered from the bondage of corruption into the glorious liberty of the children of God. ²² For we know that the whole creation groaneth and travaileth in pain together until now.

My second point has to do with the law of the seed. Laws established by righteous authority can be great in their proper place and time. There are natural laws and spiritual laws. An example of a natural law is gravity. Gravity is good—unless you have fallen from a tree.

Learning Gravity's Law

I will tell somewhat of a random little story here, to give a chance to let our minds catch up. I spent my childhood in the countryside near Brewton, Alabama, USA. I had a very good childhood with a loving family. We had our issues like most families, but as a whole, life was stable. I have one brother who is twenty-one months younger than me. We are still heavily involved in each other's lives and families. Growing up out in the country, we had many encounters with the great outdoors. We enjoyed ourselves, but had some situations that produced stories that we continue to recount even to this day. I'll share some of my stories along the way in this book to help us walk out of some of our mindsets.

This is how Yahweh keeps me firmly grounded in Him while we fly high together traversing the universe. When things in life seem to get a little complicated, I hear my Father's voice saying, "Go spend time with your grandbabies." When my wife Robbie and I have them over, they usually require all of our attention so we can't think of much else. I love it and I find it very fulfilling. It's work—but we get to give them back to their parents. At this writing, Robbie and I have eight grandchildren with another on the way. We have four grandsons and four granddaughters. They're perfect as far as Nina and Paw Paw are concerned.

I said I have a story, and here it is. When my brother and I were young teenagers, we had a camp house deep in the forest behind our home. We had many friends and relatives, and we loved staying at the old camp house. We loved it also because our only chaperone was our cousins' granddad and our great uncle, Roy. We loved him for many reasons in that he basically let us roam free. We also loved the fact that he would go to bed early and would just tell us boys to behave ourselves. It didn't hurt our feelings, either, that he was blind in one eye and almost deaf.

He had worked most of his entire life in a sawmill. There were not many lawsuits in those days, so he wasn't provided with protective gear. He was missing several fingers. It was really amazing that he had not had a major accident that could've killed him.

Looking back, though, I think he could hear better than he let on to us. Funny, huh? One night, there was a large group of us spending the night and we were a little bored, so some of the guys went for a walk. There was a long straight drive coming down to the camp. On both sides of the long dirt road were tall pines that created a beautiful canopy. Usually, the native Long Leaf pine tree doesn't have low limbs, but this type of pine had low limbs even though the tree itself is still around 75 feet tall. About ten guys had gone on the walk and a few of us stayed back.

We stayed back because we had a plan to climb the pines and jump out on the guys when they walked back. We thought it would be fun and we could scare them. It was a moonlit night, so we could pretty well see the guys in the distance, but we hid ourselves so they couldn't see us. We were on both sides of the road and we began to climb.

The guys were coming down the road much quicker than we'd expected, so we began to climb faster—too fast. I decided to go higher even though I knew that it wasn't wise with pine trees. You see, pine trees can have many dead, weak limbs along the trunk mingled with those that are alive and strong. In the daytime it was easy to see which branches were dead, but at night, not so.

I started climbing faster and higher when suddenly I felt the deadness of a limb. I tried to grab another limb, but to no avail. The law of gravity took control.

I began to fall, my back down, hitting one limb after another. Gravity was drawing me down to the earth and there was not another law or set of laws that could help me. I finally cleared the last limb and waited for impact.

I was able to lift my head enough to see one of my friends across the road looking up, trying to figure out what was going on. Suddenly, I hit and several things happened. I saw a flash of light as my head bounced off the hard ground. I hit the ground hard enough to knock the wind out of my lungs.

I jumped to my feet, trying to regain my breath in a half-run back toward the camp. As I was running, along with not being able to breathe, I tasted blood in my mouth. It was frightening. I finally began to get my breath when someone said, "Oh no: you're bleeding out of your mouth!"

I looked into a small mirror in the dimly lit room and saw blood coming out of the edge of my mouth. My first thought was that I was bleeding internally. I know it sounds funny now, but at the time, it was scary. My next thought was, "Oh no, my mother is going to be very upset!"

I was soon relieved to find out that the blood was just from me biting my tongue. One of the guys took me by motorcycle back home to check if I needed medical help or not.

I think I jarred every bone in my body. I could barely move for days and was very bruised. My mother was upset, but glad I was okay. My dad was out of town and was later informed of my fall. He didn't like it that we didn't go to the hospital to make sure there weren't more serious injuries. But we were country folk, and we didn't run to the hospital or doctor for just anything.

By the way: uncle Roy slept soundly through it all and never knew of the incident.

Gravity was not at fault, this time, for it was fulfilling its right to enforce what it is: a law of attraction. I think it is so cool that no one knows what gravity is in any fundamental way. Man understands how it works, but doesn't know what really makes it work. Gravity is a well-established law, but how is it a law?

A scientific law is: "a generalized rule to explain a body of observations in the form of a verbal or mathematical statement. Scientific laws imply a cause and effect between the observed elements and must always apply under the same conditions."[32] Another way to define a scientific law is this: a phenomenon of nature or a sequence of phenomena that are "invariable under the same conditions"—the phenomenon occurs whenever certain conditions exist or are met.[33] The definition sounds general, but there it is. Applied to gravity, it means to me that by observation, when something somehow goes up, at some point in time it will return back down.

An airplane will stay in the air as long as it has lift and thrust. Likewise, a helicopter can sustain itself airborne as long as it can maintain lift. It takes the power of the engines turning the rotor blades fast enough to create the lift effect. Part of the beauty of flight is how engineers use other laws—such as those of the effects of high pressure and low pressure over and under wings—to bring about a stable flying environment. I'm still amazed to see a large aircraft fly by. Smart and courageous people dared to look beyond the one predominant law of gravity and use that law for the good. I enjoy flying, but I also enjoy coming back to earth. Thanks to our ability to govern gravity by using additional laws of lift and thrust, we can also return home.

The law of gravity is amazing, for without it, matter couldn't exist in this dimension. Gravity holds our planet together and holds our solar system intact. Gravity holds the Milky Way galaxy that we call home intact. As a matter of fact,

32 Anne Marie Helmenstine. "What Do They Mean When They Say It's a Natural Law?" ThoughtCo. https://www.thoughtco.com/definition-of-scientific-law-605643.
33 Based on "Law," entry 15. a., in *Random House College Dictionary, Revised Edition*, New York: Random House, Inc., 1988.

all galaxies are held together by gravity. One reason scientists believe the universe is expanding is due to the observation that galaxies are moving farther apart due to gravitational expansion. This is so cool because no one really knows what makes gravity do what it does—hold things together.

However, I think we do know, and as juvenile or corny as it sounds, I believe it is the best answer. What is it? Basically, almighty God said it, and it still is. The power within His word that went out in the beginning of creation remains the same force that holds everything together today. We call it gravity.

The etymology of *gravity* has varied derivations, but one is the Latin word *gravitas*, meaning *weight*, or *heaviness*. This meaning reminds me of one of the definitions from the Hebrew word *kabowd*, glory. The Eber letters are כָּבוֹד, Kaph, Beit, Vav, and Dalet. My interpretation from the Eber definition is:

> the open hands of Yahweh's house has securely pegged creation to the doorway of Yahweh's path and purpose.

In a nutshell, Yahweh's creation is grounded to its purpose in its position and place. The elements in and around the earth, like the elements within a seed, are established and held together by His Word and it is held together by gravity—or is it His glory? Notice the last letter in the word *kabowd,* which is Dalet, the door. I believe creation is a house. All within the house have been given permission by Yahweh to exist. However, it stands at the door. Why is it at the door? It's at the door waiting to be ordered to exit the door to transform elementally and dimensionally into its desired purpose according to Yahweh's plan and blueprint. This has already happened and it is recorded in Genesis 2:19 when Adam *named* every living creature.

This glory is glorious in its dimension. As gravity does its thing, then order can be established. Creation still groans to find its original sound that it made before it was tethered to the sun and moon. How could that be, when gravity was in place? Or has it always been in place? The answer is dimensional. This may become a little mysterious, but this is why we have the Seven Spirits of the Lord available for us in this new age. We can only discern these mysteries from the tutors and governors, The Seven Spirits of the Lord, along with the tools of the Seven Thunders.

Quantum Entanglement and the Space-Time Continuum

Let us look again at the word *remaineth* from Genesis 8:22. "*While the earth remaineth, seedtime and harvest, and cold and heat, and summer and winter, and day and night shall not cease.*" In Hebrew, it is the word יוֹם or *yowm,* made up of Yod, Vav, Mem. *Yod,* in this setting speaking of day, means a beginning path to eternity. *Vav* means a tent that is pegged to the earth. The tent represents a temporary place. *Mem* speaks of a vastness of the spirit and of depths and heights. So, my view of Eber's definition of *remaineth* is

> the earth is on a temporary path that is waiting to move to
> the dimensions that are unlimited by time and space.

Have you ever heard of the scientific term *quantum entanglement?* Quantum entanglement was first observed by Albert Einstein, and it greatly challenged his thinking.

First, let's define *quantum*. "Quantum is the Latin word for *amount* and, in modern understanding, means *the smallest possible discrete unit of any physical property, such as energy or matter.*"[34] The word *quantum* and its applications can sound overly scientific and maybe even mysterious, but it is not, and it can bring mysterious things into view or perspective. *Yod,* י, in Hebrew, is synonymous with quantum. It's like a dot that can reveal the significance of a very small place. It can also point to a path or give an answer to the mysteries of a hidden place. Consider the following explanation: "In quantum physics, entangled particles remain connected so that actions performed on one affect the other, even when separated by great distances. The phenomenon so riled Albert Einstein he called it 'spooky action at a distance.' Entanglement occurs when a pair of particles, such as photons, interact physically."[35]

Spiritually, quantum entanglement is not spooky at all, for it gives reference to what Yahshua referred to in John 17. The entire chapter of John 17 speaks of an entanglement in which what happens in one happens instantaneously in the other. This is a joining by the Spirit in which time and space cannot determine the outcome of the move of the Spirit. If you will, spiritual quantum entanglement can be determined dimensionally not only instantaneously, but it can also help us understand how we can engage the beginning to the finishing. It allows us to see creation, and it helps us engage with what is on earth as it is in Heaven. This can only be discerned by the Spirit and through engaging the Seven Spirits of the Lord as they teach us these great dimensional matters.

34 Margaret Rouse. "What is Quantum? – Definition from WhatIs.com." May 2016. Accessed June 14, 2018. https://whatis.techtarget.com/definition/quantum
35 Tate, Karl. "How Quantum Entanglement Works." Live Science. April 8, 2013. https://www.livescience.com/28550-how-quantum-entanglement-works-infographic.html.

Have you ever heard of the scientific term *space-time continuum*? Please think about the following example from your spirit mind of Christ: "Einstein's theory of special relativity created a fundamental link between space and time. The universe can be viewed as having three space dimensions — up/down, left/right, forward/backward — and one time dimension. This 4-dimensional space is referred to as the space-time continuum."[36]

In the 2014 epic science fiction film *Interstellar*, we witnessed the effects of spacetime and what happens in wormholes and black holes. I loved the movie because it spoke of dimensions and time in a unique way. Taking place in the future, the movie portrays an Earth where a global crop blight and second Dust Bowl are slowly rendering the planet uninhabitable. Professor Brand (Michael Caine), a brilliant NASA physicist, is working on plans to save mankind by transporting Earth's population to a new home via a wormhole. First, however, Brand must send former NASA pilot Cooper (Matthew McConaughey) and a team of researchers through the wormhole and across the galaxy to find out which of three planets could be mankind's new home. SPOILER ALERT: If you plan to see the movie yourself, then skip the next paragraph.

When Cooper has to enter a blackhole, everything changes in time. Black holes eliminate time due to their extreme gravitational pull. The mission, in Earth's relative time, took many years. Cooper had been very close to his daughter and had left on his mission when she was young. When he is finally able to return to his daughter, she is already near death at the

---

36   Andrew Zimmerman Jones and Daniel Robbins. "String Theory Unifies Space and Time." https://www.dummies.com/education/science/physics/string-theory-unifies-space-and-time/

age of 86. He was technically well over a hundred years old, but Cooper had only aged by 2 years due to the effects of the gravitational pull of the black hole. By the time he returned, Earth had become uninhabitable but his daughter and others were now living on an "advanced spacefaring civilization" that they had built in space. Basically, they had built their own Earth within its own environment, but it was no longer a sphere. This movie had a physicist as one of the executive producers, Kip Thorne. He attempted to keep the movie as scientifically accurate as possible while keeping it interesting as Hollywood likes to do. I loved the movie.

Yahweh sometimes uses the movie industry to bring home a point or assist us in waking up to our position and place. This has to happen because the church has either been stuck in a religious place or lost in the past. I know it is obvious, but most of the movie industry is a waste of time and can possibly cause your IQ to drop. (That last part was a joke, but maybe there is some truth to it.)

A *scientist* is "someone who systematically gathers and uses research and evidence, making a hypothesis and testing it, to gain and share understanding and knowledge." (Definition available at sciencecouncil.org). A scientist can be further defined by how they go about their research. For example, they can be classified by their use of statistics (statisticians) or data (data scientists),what they're seeking understanding of, such as the elements in the universe (chemists, geologists, etc.) or the stars in the sky (astronomers), or where they apply their science, such as in the food industry (food scientist).

There have been many amazing men and women of science and math in the past and present that have perceived

Creation in their own way. Let us take a brief look at just a few of them and whether each of them believed or believes in God.

Historic scientist:

- Leonardo da Vinci, 1452-1519: polymath (believer)
- Isaac Newton, 1643-1727: mathematician, astronomer, theologian, author and physicist (believer)
- James Clerk Maxwell, 1831-1879: mathematical physics (believer)
- Nikola Tesla, 1856-1943: electrical engineer, mechanical engineer, physicist (believer)
- Max Planck, 1858-1947: theoretical physicist (believer)
- Marie Curie, 1867-1934: physicist and chemist (atheist)
- Albert Einstein, 1879-1955: theoretical physicist (uncertain but possibly an agnostic)
- Wernher von Braun, 1912-1977: aerospace engineer and space architect (believer)

Modern day scientists:

- James Watson, 1928: molecular biologist, geneticist, zoologist (atheist)
- Elizabeth Blackburn, 1948: molecular and cellular biologist (unclear as a believer, but no signs in any articles and research says she is)
- Timothy Berners-Lee, 1955: computer science (more than likely agnostic but rejected Christianity despite continuing belief in the possibility of a god)
- Stephen Hawking, 1942-2018: theoretical physicist, cosmologist, and author (atheist)

Although this is a very small account of the large number of prominent scientists that have lived, I still believe that we have a potential pattern between modern day scientists and scientists prior to the 1950s. I know that those whom we consider "scientists" have been around since the beginning. I've glimpsed a pattern of those living prior to WWII comparable to those living afterward.

Some things have happened since then that may have desensitized us to the Creator. I think it is obvious that the exposure to the ages of the last seventy years have been a great contributor. The Christian churches of the last centuries have mishandled or greatly misinterpreted the words of Yahshua when He said that we are not of this world. There are many reference points in scripture, but the one that stands out to me is John 17:14–16. The church has never engaged by the Spirit to lead the world, but has given place for the world to lead us or, more frighteningly, our children. This lack of engagement to lead has given way to an atheistic society, or an "anything goes" society, and a weakling church. Changes to this world have come and are in the works now for a greater revealing and exchange. Let us look at some of the markers.

There are spiritual ages and natural ages that chronicle changes that have developed due to discoveries and development of these discoveries. These changes, at first, take courage and a boldness to break through the status quo and standards that have kept a cycle in place. Once it begins to take hold, through determination by a few, then the age changes. There are three marked natural ages of the last seventy years that have enabled most everyone on our planet to have access to information, be it true or untrue.

1. The Ages of the Digital Revolution, which is also known as the Third Industrial Revolution. It was the shift from mechanical and analogue electronic technology to digital electronics. (The late 1950s–the late 1970s)

2. The Computer Age (Started in the 70s until now)

3. The Information Age (Started around the 70s until now)

The new Industrial Revolution is the IoT (Internet of Things) and AI (Artificial Intelligence). We, the family of Yahweh, should be not only be aware of the age change, but harness their possibilities. We, the believers, must be seated in these arenas and fearlessly, joyfully and respectfully guide them. Although believers have used and taken some advantage of all three aforementioned ages, we were far behind those who seized it with all of their hearts and finances.

I have had the distinct pleasure and honor, because of the field of study of the company that I have founded, to be affiliated with a number of scientists. I appreciate their dedicated work ethic, focus and brilliance. The ones I've been around are primarily physicists or mathematicians working with science. They respect facts for what they are: facts that can be proven.

I have discovered that these scientists are intrigued with any new way of thinking that engages a potential outcome for advancement. Most of them believe in sharing through the papers that they write up about new ways of discovery. In the scientific community that I've been a part of, I have been shocked to note that they prefer not being called by the title *doctor*. Their names and credentials are listed on their identification and business cards, but they prefer you use their first names. However, this is not the case at professional presentations among their peers. They may not have taken any notice of these things, but it is something I've noticed from my experiences being around them. Do they have egos? Like most any profession, I'm sure pride and egos are there, but I've been pleasantly surprised that I have yet to notice any. Respect for each other is the key to their further success, accomplishments and discoveries. They realize that they need each other. Many of them pinpoint one specific area of study and attempt to master it. There is a true lesson in that alone.

I have, by the Spirit, met and have an ongoing dialogue with James Clerk Maxwell. I know that sounds weird, and in the last ages I would have called myself a kook. The blessings and treasures we have been awarded in these amazing ages of peace have enabled us to engage with the cloud of witnesses. They took treasure to the grave, but the grave and death no longer have a sting. Thanks be to Yahshua for making a way out. The veil is rent!

James was an outspoken believer in his day, but was basically rejected by the religious folks of his day because he was a scientist. He was challenged by many of his scientific peers for his desire to participate in the church. He died at the young age of 48 and took with him secrets and mysteries that he knew didn't deserve to be revealed in that day. I have good news! Yahshua has overcome the world and has become a testimony that the grave cannot withhold the treasures that it has held since the beginning.

In this great new age of peace that we have now entered, these scientific terms are not meant to bind our minds. These terms are meant to assist in our embracing of the overall reality of what we are by the Spirit. *"For now we see through a glass darkly; but then face to face: now I know in part; but then shall I know even as I also am known"* (1 Cor. 13:12). This scripture mysteriously speaks of a position of identity in time and space. When is *now*, and when is *then*? I call on the Second Thunder to assist me in retrieving the revelation of this mysterious expression.[37]

Many mysteries are presented to us in scripture. A mystery works in two ways. One way is through the obvious language or picture that presents a hint or teaser of what might be beyond the literal words, numbers, picture, etc. The second way a mystery may be presented in scripture is by appearing to be normal in words, numbers or pictures, but something about it just isn't normal or common. It's as if the mystery is right there in plain view, but it is hidden to those unaware or not engaged. Mysteries, to me, are like personalities of a revelation.

The Mystery of Now and Then

Let us look into the mysteries that are presented in this amazing verse of First Corinthians 13:12. Read it again:

> *For now we see through a glass darkly; but then face to face: now I know in part; but then shall I know even as I also am known.*

---

37 The Second Thunder reveals mysteries, secrets, and riddles. See Chapter 8, "The Seven Thunders," pp. 88-92 in *Come Up Here: The Place of Our Original Intent,* Mobile, AL: Scrolls of Zebulon, 2016.

Consider the positions of time mentioned in the verse: now, then. When is *now* and when is *then*? The mystery is when is *now* and what happens that makes *then* so different and fulfilled? *Now*, of course, is the present state of being. The position of now reveals a posture of incompleteness. The good news is that in the now-position, the act of seeing, stated as "we see" in the verse, is still being engaged. You first must see.

The desire to see the rest of the picture requires more. To realize the fulfillment of *then* you must look at the picture from a different position or angle. In other words, it's time to move! The question may be how, when, and where we move? Keep repositioning yourself until you see everything clearly. If you are unable to change your position, then call on the Holy Ghost. It's imperative to be filled with the Holy Ghost. As you draw upon His never ending source, engage with the Seven Spirits of the Lord. They will assist you in what is needed. Remember: *"It is the glory of God to conceal a thing: but the honour of kings is to search out a matter"* (Prov. 25:2).

When you face yourself and no longer see problems or blemishes, even though they attempt to speak louder than anything else, then you will see Yahweh in you and you in Yahweh. When this is a reality to you, the gospel according to Luke 1:37, *"For with God nothing shall be impossible,"* will become your Word.

In order for us to be the revealers of the Romans 8 man, we must engage with the reality of Yahweh's desires. If you are serious about doing the will of our Father, then fear not. Easier said than done? Not really: just change positions and listen to the appropriate voice and not the voice of caution. Remember the reference to the still small voice?

¹¹ And he said, Go forth, and stand upon the mount before the Lord. And, behold, the Lord passed by, and a great and strong wind rent the mountains, and brake in pieces the rocks before the Lord; but the Lord was not in the wind: and after the wind an earthquake; but the Lord was not in the earthquake:

¹² And after the earthquake a fire; but the Lord was not in the fire: and after the fire a still small voice.

¹³ And it was so, when Elijah heard it, that he wrapped his face in his mantle, and went out, and stood in the entering in of the cave. … (1 Kings 19:11–13)

Do not misinterpret the still small voice. Let's call on the steward of the Hebrew language, Eber, for the depths to this very important apocalypse. The phrase *a still* comes from the Hebrew *dĕmamah*, דְּמָמָה, made up of the letters Dalet, Mem, Mem, Hey. Eber's translation is:

> The breath of Yahweh witnesses within the depths of chaos and reveals that the door is open for communication.

The word *small*, or in Hebrew, *daq*, דַּק, comes from the Hebrew letters Dalet, Quph. Eber's translation describes the size of

> the door that opens to opportunity is measured from Zion's inner portals.

The word *voice* or *qowl*, קוֹל, comes from the Hebrew letters Quph, Yud, Lamed. Eber's translation is:

> the frequency that traverses all creation to connect all timelines to a place and position.

This translation sounds like quantum entanglement to me. Yahweh's voice is capable of transcending time and the cycle factor. Next we'll look at a familiar story from the Gospels that illustrates this dimensional transcendence.

Dimensional Reality Shown through a Fig Tree

Do you remember the story of the fig tree that had only produced leaves? Many sermons have been preached to try explain the bizarre yet awesome account of the sudden demise of a fig tree that appeared to be doing what is otherwise normal. We find two similar yet different accounts of the story in Matthew and Mark's gospels.

Matthew 21:17–22

> *¹⁷ And he left them, and went out of the city into Bethany; and he lodged there. ¹⁸ Now in the morning as he returned into the city, he hungered. ¹⁹ And when he saw the fig tree in the way, he came to it, and found nothing thereon, but leaves only, and said unto it, Let no fruit grow on thee henceforward for ever. And presently the fig tree withered away. ²⁰ And when the disciples saw it, they marveled, saying, How soon is the fig tree withered away! ²¹ Jesus answered and said unto them, Verily I say unto you, if you have faith, and doubt not, ye shall not only do this which is done to the fig tree, but also if you shall say unto this mountain, Be thou removed, and be thou cast into the sea; it shall be done. ²² And all things, whatsoever ye shall ask in prayer, believing, ye shall receive.*

Mark 11:11-14; 19–26

* And Jesus entered into Jerusalem, and into the temple: and when he had looked round about upon all things, and now the even tide was come, he went out unto Bethany with the twelve. ¹² And on the morrow, when they were come from Bethany, he was hungry: ¹³ And seeing a fig tree afar off having leaves, he came, if haply he might find any thing thereon: and when he came to it, he found nothing but leaves; for the time of figs was not yet. ¹⁴ And Jesus answered and said unto it, No man eat fruit of thee hereafter for ever. And his disciples heard it.*

...

¹⁹ And when even was come, he went out of the city. ²⁰ And in the morning, as they passed by, they saw the fig tree dried up from the roots. ²¹ And Peter calling to remembrance saith unto him, Master, behold, the fig tree which thou cursedst is withered away. ²² And Jesus answering saith unto them, Have faith in God. ²³ For verily I say unto you, That whosoever shall say unto this mountain, Be thou removed and cast into the sea; and shall bot doubt in his heart, but shall believe that those things which he saith shall come to pass; he shall have whatever he saith. ²⁴ Therefore I say unto you, what things soever ye desire, when ye pray, believe that ye receive them, and ye shall have them. ²⁵ and when ye stand praying, forgive, if you have ought against any: that your Father also which is in heaven may forgive you your trespasses. ²⁶ but if ye do not forgive, neither will your Father which is in heaven forgive your trespasses.

The fig tree was just doing what its cell memory was programmed to do. So, what set off the pronouncement of death to this seemingly-innocent fig tree?

Note several points from these combined accounts and their similarities and differences.

- Both accounts declare Yahshua was in Jerusalem, the house or city of peace.

    Jeru- represents not only the house, but the city. *Salem* means peace, but also refers to a state of completeness, a lack of division, harmony. It also can mean *whole* and *safe*. I encourage you to study the depths of the living Hebrew letters that better reveal this ancient name.[38]

- Both accounts agree that Yahshua left from Jerusalem headed to Bethany.

    Bethany means house of figs. *Beth* means house. It was called the house of figs. Figs represent many things in Israel, from Israel itself, to an abundance of blessings, to restoration and healing.

- Both accounts agree that Yahshua was hungry.

    Anything and everything in the life of Yahshua was significant. His hunger is indicative of a normal need to be nourished. We should be reminded that He had physical needs just as we do. His hunger was no doubt physical, but it also represents, to me, a sense of need for the earth and its life to recognize the King's approach.

38 To study the individual letters and their meanings and applications, see A. Smith, T. Bowen, E. Corley, Y.A. Butler, & D. Cook, *Friends of Eber: A Reference Guide to the Living Letters of the Hebrew Alphabet* (Mobile, AL: Scrolls of Zebulon, 2016).

- Both accounts note that Yahshua saw a fig tree at a long distance.

  This indicates dimensions of distance and time. I'm sure you can picture it as I do. Yahshua and the disciples stroll along together on a stony dirt path, and Yahshua recognizes the leaves of a fig tree in the distance. It is going to be a while before they have their encounter with the tree. In our mind's eye, we see figs on the tree. After you complete the distance to change positions to be where the fig tree is located, you obtain what you need. It will take some time due to the distance.

  Now, let us look from another view. The King of glory was walking a path that would take a certain amount of the earth spinning and moving around the sun before He could find Himself in the same place as the fig tree. It sounds odd, but it is true. As we will see in some of the next points, what is being challenged here in this story is not just a fig tree with no fruit, but He's challenging time and space. I'll explain as we go.

- Both accounts speak of Yahshua seeing nothing but leaves only.

  I grew up in the country near farmland and a forest, so I know a little about plant life and trees. Plants and trees grow seasonally, depending on the position of the earth's rotation. Close proximity to the equator eliminates some seasons, but those areas have other cycles that seeds respond to in order to produce. Every tree and plant has its own peculiarities of color, shape, and size. Much like anything that is of a seed—including our physical bodies—we all have a certain look.

- Yahshua knew the look of a fig tree. He knew the shape of the tree and the leaves, for the fig tree and its leaves are distinct. The leaves are on the tree to make a way for the sole purpose of the tree, and that is for it to produce fruit. In a normal cycle of seasons, the tree needs enough nourishment from the leaves to produce the goal of the tree which is a distinct fruit which then ensures its perpetuity. The leaves themselves are amazing creations which assist in nourishment and growth. The fig tree doesn't have many leaves, but the leaves on most species are large. The leaves work from above as the roots work from beneath. One brings nutrients from the earth and the other from the Heavens. Leaves are basically receivers of light, photons. Leaves have an amazing ability to take the photons into the tree branches and synthesize them together with the nutrients that ascend from the roots. Then the DNA of the tree is activated. This is a normal process and requires many factors that come to pass over time.

- Both accounts agree that Yahshua pronounced that *"no man eat fruit of thee hereafter for ever"* and *"the fig tree withered away."*

   Many things happened and began to happen when Yahshua made this declaration. He pronounced a curse on the fig tree that was full of life. The curse was that the tree now can't do what it was designed to do. He removed its purpose.

Wow! Can we stop here and see how this lines up with so many lost souls on our planet? When we lose our purpose, we have lost our reason to live. But don't only notice what He said; also notice what He didn't say. He didn't say that it couldn't bear fruit, but that no one would ever eat of the fruit of the tree. He also said it was going to be forever, meaning there was no other season of time where things could change. The soul of the tree was removed from its purpose.

- Matthew's account of when the evidence of the pronouncement would manifest appeared to be immediate: *"And presently the fig tree withered away."*

    It's a mystery why the two accounts of this incident are so different in some points. Why? There are many logical answers and one or most of them may be true, but I find it interesting that both versions from Matthew and Mark made it to print. I believe that dimensionally both are correct. I'm not trying to justify the discrepancy—I'm speaking dimensionally. We see things in a linear fashion most of the time, but with Yahshua and Yahweh things are multidimensional.

- Mark's account of the manifestation and the observed outcome was very different and is found in verses 19–21.

Mark states that it was in the morning when they passed back by, that they saw the tree dried up from the roots. Matthew's account states that the fig tree withered away immediately. Later Mark notes, *"Peter calling to remembrance saith unto him, Master, behold, the fig tree which thou cursed is withered away"* (v. 21). Engage with both of their accounts. Which account fits with you? It could be both. This may be confusing to some, but when you engage the dimensions, you will get what I'm saying.

Here are a few more points to consider from the encounter with the fig tree.

The fig tree should have perceived the King's coming.	Perception
The fig tree should have discerned the King's heart, need, and desire.	Discernment
The fig tree had everything within it to produce immediately if it didn't associate with the pattern of the cycle of death.	Association
When Yahshua was asked about the demise of the fig tree, He focused not on what happened naturally, but on His faith. Yahshua even seemed excited at what His faith had done. Faith sees past cycles and into dimensions that render the desire of the faithful as long as it is aligned with the Father. The faith of Yahshua demanded an outcome or judgment for justice's sake.	Faith Prevails
There is no mention of Yahshua fulfilling His hunger other than His faith brought his fulfillment.	Fulfillment

Concerning where we are dimensionally positioned now, the entire account of the demise of the fig tree is prophetic. If we see cycles of life and death as our path, then we will not set forth the outcome that is desired by Yahweh: justice. If our faith requires fruit, even out of season, and the earth doesn't respond, then our dimensional faith will require the dimension that is housing the fig tree and its cycle to respond. If not, then I believe the dimensions will collapse in on each other.

What does that mean? There is a dimension that maintains a place of provision for the cyclic seed in the fig tree. That dimension collapsed in and around the tree causing it to remain normal according to its season even when The Christ called for it to bear fruit. The faith of Yahshua required a dimensional shift that operates from Heaven instead of earth. Wow!

Breaking Life and Death Cycles: Who Are You in Glory?

How do we break the cycles of life and death? Basically, we must have the faith to embrace the life and/or light of Yahweh. The cycles of life and death are broken when you are born again, but I've discovered that many who are born again remain slaves by association to one of the slave systems.[39] I'm convinced that obtaining and engaging with the mind of Christ is the key. Being born again gives you the total right to receive this great gift, life everlasting, through Ruach Kodesh, the Holy Ghost.

I have some questions that may shake you. If they do shake you, then maybe you need to know why you are shaken. If you feel very guarded about these questions, then you may be insecure in what you believe. The challenge is not to offend, but for us to be open about a few things in us who believe. The goal of these questions is not to upset, but to help shore up what we believe and why we believe it. This will enable us

---

39 See my discussion of "The Four Slave Systems," in *Come Up Here: The Place of Our Original Intent* (Mobile, AL: Scrolls of Zebulon, 2016), 170-184.

to mark a place in time where we back up what we believe. Maybe we can draw from this as we proceed into this amazing place of Zion. I believe confidence is a great thing, and once you are established in what you believe, confidence should be present. Those who become cocky or arrogant in their faith have lost touch with the reality of the humility that's within the love and salvation of Yahweh. Never settle with being a professional church-goer or professional Christian. Be the sons and daughters who resemble your Father in His love, forgiveness, and amazing peace.

When I ask the following questions, please try not to instantly answer with canned, religious answers. I'm not saying we don't believe those answers: I'm saying to wait for a moment to establish your position. I have many questions that are not meant to offend but to provoke in order to bring a better establishment of what you already believe. I encourage you to write out your answers to this self-test so that you may see them. Then, read them aloud.

Salvation: Questions

1. What happened to you when you were saved?

2. What were you saved from, and what were you saved to?

3. When were you born again?

4. Are being *saved* and being *born again* the same thing?

5. How can you prove that you are born again, and what is your evidence that you have been born again?

6. What did Yahshua mean in John 3:5 that *"unless you are born of the water and of the Spirit, you cannot enter the kingdom"*? (Note: *Spirit* is *pneuma*—a current of air, breath or breath of Christ's spirit.)

7. From 1 Peter 1:23, what is the incorruptible seed?

8. What happened to you when you were born again?

9. Did you feel something when you were born again, and if so, what?

10. Did you have a *knowing,* and if so, can you explain?

11. What was your spiritual experience like?

12. What does it mean to be crucified with Christ?

13. What does it mean to be buried with Him in baptism and raised with Him in newness of life?

My challenge to us is not meant to discourage, but to shake us into the realization that perhaps in some cases we have settled for something of a feeling only. I celebrate the knowing in our hearts, and sometimes that may be all we have. In many cases, it is all we need.

I do believe in this great new place of Up Here in Zion that we must be born again. We may have some evidence that we are of Him, but we may have settled for much less than what He desires in us through being born again. Peace that passes understanding is evidence, but it is not overwhelming evidence to the world. Many eastern religious orders claim peace. So where could the evidence be?

Tired of the questions? Me, too. I will comment on some of the questions, but I believe that you are meant to work them all out by the Helper, Ruach Kodesh, Holy Spirit.

Salvation: My Answers, and Yours

1. My experience occurred when I had been tracked down by God and I faced Him. When I faced Him, all I saw or felt was His love, acceptance and forgiveness. In what way did he track me down? He was everywhere I looked, and I heard His voice calling unto me. One day, I finally answered. I have found that many have a difficult time explaining what we felt when we were saved. You have to experience it in order to get what it is all about. The love that only Yahweh can give is what I felt and peace entered my lost and restless soul. I finally realized that I had been lost, then suddenly His amazing love is what found me!

2. We were saved from ourselves in our very self-serving and limited conscientiousness and, of course, from death. We were saved to His glorious presence and love. We no longer were ever meant to continue to wander in search of our place and the meaning of our being. Our wanderings were an acknowledgment of being lost without God and a desire to find and embrace Him.

3. Let's look at the natural process of being born. The pressure of birthing through the birth canal leads to the crowning of the head, then comes the shoulders, which are followed by the rest of the body. The two pressure points are the head and then the shoulders. They both speak of authority. I think most everyone would agree that the head speaks of authority and where the crown fits, but what about the shoulders?

Isaiah 9:6 gives us the answer: *"For unto us a child is born, unto us a son is given, and the government shall be upon his shoulder…"* The authority relating to the head associates with the Christ. Consider Ephesians 4:15, *"…speaking the truth in love, [we] may grow up into him in all things, which is the head, Christ."* The head is where we think and make our decisions. The shoulders represent carrying the burden that holds up the frame. It represents the strength of authority.

I love the story of when King David was bringing the Ark of the covenant back home. The Philistines had captured the Ark and it caused them some serious problems. Put it this way: the Preparation H company would have made a killing in profits. The Philistines were cursed with hemorrhoids for capturing the Ark of the Lord. The story is found in First Samuel chapters 5–7. The story of Uzzah is found in Second Samuel 6 where David had the idea of bringing the Ark in the same way the Philistines had sent it out from them, on a cart. As the story goes, Uzzah, who was one of the men bringing the Ark back on a cart, reached out his hand to stabilize the Ark so that it wouldn't fall off the cart. This action cost him his life, for he was struck dead. His name means "strength of the flesh of man." His intention might normally be considered reasonable and even honorable, but he broke protocol. As a matter of fact, the entire thing was wrong, for everyone involved broke protocol. So, death occurred. The event shocked and offended David. The Ark was taken to the house of Obed-Edom where it remained for three months. The blessing of Yahweh was so great upon Obed-Edom that David enquired of the priests what went wrong before and what was the correct way to carry the Ark. The Ark represented many things, but primarily the blessings of Yahweh. It was provision for purpose through His mercy. The priests revealed that the Ark was to be moved only by the priests and on their shoulders. The hand, in this case Uzzah's, represented the strength of man, and the shoulders of the priests represented the strength of Yahweh. So *born again*, to me, represents not only being saved from death unto life, but it represents being born into the family of Yahweh. Yahshua made the way possible by his shed blood. I was born again when I took on another form—it was when I took on the image and likeness of Yahshua the Christ.

4. Being saved and being born again are not the same, but being saved brings you to a place to become born again. I see it as if the words spoken about us, mentioned in Psalms 139, have been saved from nothingness. *"Thine eyes did see my substance, yet being unperfect; and in thy book all my members were written, when in continuance were fashioned, when as yet there was none of them"* (Psalm 139:16). Becoming born again enables those words to be realized for eternity.

5. The proof and evidence of my being born again occur as I become His image and likeness and as I make the word tangible in the now.

6. The water represents conformity to a vessel. It is not only the water grave of baptism, but that which can uphold a vessel and can be contained within it. Water, when governed, is a life-source, but when it is not properly governed, water is a tremendous destroyer. Likewise, when Yahshua mentions the Spirit, I believe he is referencing the breath which must be housed and governed from a vessel. Naturally, both the water and the breath or air operate in similar ways. Water is made up of two parts hydrogen and one part oxygen, H_2O. The air we breathe is oxygen. So, in a nutshell, it has to do with authority recognized on earth (water) and of Heaven (the Spirit or breath).

7. The incorruptible seed does not house the life cycle of death within it. Revelation 2:7 states, *"He that hath an ear, let him hear what the Spirit says to churches; To him that overcometh will I give to eat of the tree of life, which is in the paradise of God."* This seed has the DNA of Yahweh within it. My friend Ian Clayton says that our double helix DNA is meant to transform into a triple strand. I agree, for Yahweh builds in threes. I used to think the double helix represented what we call Jacob's ladder. I believe it is a good analogy of the spiraling staircase, but this DNA is not complete and cycles life and death.

8. I believe that when you are born again everything changes, but all changes will not be realized until our minds fully associate and identify with our new eternal

and everlasting being of life in Christ (see Romans 8:1–17).

9. (This should be your personal account, and I encourage you to rehearse often what happened when you were born again.)

10. I had and have a knowing in all my being that a wonderful change came into me and the amazing acceptance into the family of God occurred.

11. (This again is personal: write it down that you may rehearse it.)

12. Galatians 2:20 is a familiar scripture that we quote often, but it has great depth to it. *"I am crucified with Christ: nevertheless I live; yet not I, but Christ liveth in me: and the life which I now live in the flesh I live by the faith of the Son of God, who loved me, and gave himself for me."* Yahshua's prayer recorded in John 17 helps us to see that when we are in Him and he is in us, we take on all that He has overcome. Did we earn it? It is not about earning it, for it is a gift. I believe that our spirit-man carries His scars which represent the covenant scars from the crucifixion. If we were crucified with Him then we are likewise raised with Him.

> *³ Know ye not, that so many of us as were baptized into Jesus Christ were baptized into his death? ⁴ Therefore we are buried with him by baptism into death: that like as Christ was raised up from the dead by the glory of the Father, even so we also should walk in newness of life. ⁵ For if we have*

been planted together in the likeness of his death, we shall be also in the likeness of his resurrection: ⁶ Knowing this, that our old man is crucified with him, that the body of sin might be destroyed, that henceforth we should not serve sin. ⁷ For he that is dead is freed from sin. ⁸ Now if we be dead with Christ, we believe that we shall also live with him: ⁹ Knowing that Christ being raised from the dead dieth no more; death hath no more dominion over him. ¹⁰ For in that he died, he died unto sin once: but in that he liveth, he liveth unto God. (Romans 6: 3–10)

13. I believe the answer to this question, previously read from Romans 6, is for our faith to rise and engage with the strengths of who He is in us. This is easier said than done. I believe I know why. It is believing that we are truly His family and carry His likeness through the path He has prepared for us. It's our place and our identity.

The revealing of who we are in our glory cannot be realized in creation until we first realize it in ourselves. It's time to shake off all the effects of the old ages past and engage with who we are in the dimensions that were designed for us. Let us no longer live in a dimension that doesn't recognize us or our sound. Rather, we need to come Up Here into Zion and begin living the way we are designed to live forever within Him.

5

CHOSHEK—THE PLACE OF HIDDEN TREASURES

O ur Father is light. First John 1:5 proclaims, *"God is light."* In Psalm 18:11, Yahweh, the God of light, shrouds Himself in darkness: *"He made darkness his secret place; his pavilion round about him were dark waters and thick clouds of the skies."* This darkness is a place called *Choshek,* and it is an unusual and amazing place. It is a dark place, and like the letter Ghah some consider it to be of wickedness. This perception of darkness as wickedness is correct if you do not have permission to see and engage Choshek. But if you have permission, you'll see something different.

I believe Choshek is a place of hidden treasures. It's the place of lost, stolen, and forfeited treasures. What kind of treasures? Gold, silver, and precious stones? Possibly, but in reality the treasures are most anything considered precious. Primarily, the treasure is the Word of Yahweh held captive. Who holds His Word captive? I don't believe it is the devil. It is the Word itself being held captive by itself.

Confused? Let me explain. Maybe it is better said that the Word—the treasure—is not held in captivity, but rather it will not release itself until it hears and sees the sound. Treasure can't be fooled into releasing itself by an incorrect sound or improper appearance. I've always loved and have been drawn to Psalm 89. Verse 15 states, *"Blessed is the people that know the joyful sound: they shall walk, O Lord, in the light of thy countenance."* Verse 14 reads, *"Justice and judgment are the habitation of thy throne: mercy and truth shall go before thy face."* As my friends Ian Clayton and Grant and Samantha Mahoney say: "We must stay within our mobile throne room of Zion." I love it! We are not stationary, but we move in and out of Choshek, from within our throne rooms, from within Mount Zion, to discover the depths and execute judgment for justice. We are redeemers, for we are seated with Christ in not only Heavenly places but within Choshek.

I first discovered Choshek while preparing a decree.[40] In the decree, I used the 23rd letter, Ghah, from the Hebrew alphabet. As I searched it out, I found the path of light that spirals from Ghah through Ayin, the 16th letter. Once I go through this letter, Ayin, I find hidden letters that ascend and descend. There are twelve of them that represent the four corners and the up and down of creation's dimensions and the spiritual dimensions. These dimensions work together for our purpose. They look like seats that angle in the six different directions of the north, south, east, west, the up and the down. There is much to Choshek. I am just beginning to enquire of its uniqueness and rules of order. I look forward to the adventure.

---

40   For more on decrees, see Chapter 9, "Decrees and Declarations from Up Here," pp. 165-198 in *Come Up Here: The Place of Our Original Intent.* Mobile, AL: Scrolls of Zebulon, 2016.

The first scripture that caught my attention regarding Choshek was Genesis 1:5, *"And God called the light Day, and the darkness he called Night. And the evening and the morning were the first day."* The Seven Spirits of The Lord called to my attention three words: *Day, darkness,* and *Night.* I looked into their Hebrew names.

- *Day* is *yowm,* spelled Yud, Vav, Mem, יוֹם. Yowm is full revelation and its glory.

- *Darkness* is *Choshek,* spelled Chet, Shin, Khaf, חֹשֶׁךְ. It's a place of the hidden things that are kept from being revealed.

- *Night* is *layil,* spelled Lamed, Yud, Lamed, ליל. Layil has a related word *luwl,* spelled Lamed, Vav, Lamed. Layil and luwl together are the spiraling staircase of the night sky that guides the way into and out of Choshek.

Other scriptures engage the name Choshek, including 80 different scriptures relating to the mysterious place. *Strong's Concordance,* H2822, defines Choshek as "dark, darkness or obscurity."

I hope that you are curious enough to search out all the scriptural references to Choshek. If you are also inclined to read commentaries on Choshek and other words like layil, you will find the usual, commonplace interpretations. The commentaries that I have read are of the last ages and definitely not of the ages of peace.

As you search out the references, you will find Isaiah 5:20, which warns, *"Woe unto them that call evil good, and good evil; that put darkness for light, and light for darkness; that put bitter for sweet, and sweet for bitter!"* Commentaries on this scripture interpret from the usual view that this is strictly speaking of wickedness and associate the darkness literally known as *Choshek* as evil. But the ages changed, and for those who heard the invitation to come Up Here, our perspective of most everything changed. In the last ages, the dimensions were associated with war, thus the commentaries are correct from that perspective. But to us who have heard the joyful sound from within Zion and have ascended, everything looks and sounds very different. What I see and what I hear now resembles redemption of life: it does not resemble death, evil, and wickedness. Are death, evil and wickedness still present in the earth? Certainly, for now, but not in the dimensions of Up Here in Zion.

I love Habakkuk 2:1-3 and its interpretation from inside Zion.

> *¹ I will stand upon my watch, and set me upon the tower, and will watch to see what he will say unto me, and what I shall answer when I am reproved.*
>
> *² And the Lord answered me, and said, Write the vision, and make it plain upon tables, that he may run that readeth it.*
>
> *³ For the vision is yet for an appointed time, but at the end it shall speak, and not lie: though it tarry, wait for it; because it will surely come, it will not tarry.*

Along with Isaiah 5:20, this scripture must be interpreted from inside Zion. If not, then the strength of religion from the last war ages will prevail to bind our minds once again and keep us from engaging with the treasures that await us.

Interpreting Habakkuk 2:1–3 by Eber from Zion

Let us look into Habakkuk 2:1–3 from within their meaning as Eber and his friends interpret.

Verse 1

I will stand	Hebrew *amad*, derived from the living letters Ayin, Mem, Dalet. Eber describes his friends, saying,
	"I understand the importance to see from the portal and from within the depths of my inheritance. I will perceive the paths of the dimensions."
upon my watch,	Hebrew *mishmereth*, derived from the living letters Mem, Shin, Mem, Resh, Tav. Eber describes his friends, saying,
	"I am reminded to hold onto the fact that my supply is from the original intent so that I may finish."
and set	Hebrew *yatsab*, derived from the living letters Yod, Tsade, Beyt. Eber describes his friends, saying,
	"Seated in Righteousness, safe and secure,"
me upon the tower,	Hebrew *matsowr*, derived from the living letters Mem, Tsade, Vav, Resh. Eber describes his friends, saying,
	"I am well established in my mobile throne as I join my original intent."

| and will watch | Hebrew *tsaphah,* derived from the living letters Tsade, Pey, Hey. Eber describes his friends, saying, |

"In the path of righteousness and from this speaking place I will breathe as upon a glass."

| to see | Hebrew *ra'ah,* derived from the living letters Resh, Aleph, Hey. Eber describes his friends, saying, |

"I will look within time, lowing the frequency of Heaven and I breathe what I see into existence."

| what he will say | Hebrew *dabar,* derived from the living letters Dalet, Beyt, Resh. Eber describes his friends, saying, |

"As the portal of Heaven prepares to speak knowledge of secret places,"

| unto me, and what I shall answer | Hebrew *shuwb,* derived from the living letters Shin, Vav, Beyt. Eber describes his friends, saying, |

"I embrace the opportunity to ascend and descend from my speaking place,"

Verse 2

| And the Lord | Hebrew *Yahweh,* derived from the living letters Yod, Hey, Vav, Hey. Eber describes his friends, saying, |

"And I AM the breath of life that connects and joins the living."

answered	Hebrew *'anah,* derived from the living letters Ayin, Nun, Hey. Eber describes his friends, saying,

"I AM the portal that stands tall to breathe my word."

me, and said,	Hebrew *'amar,* derived from the living letters Aleph, Mem, Resh. Eber describes his friends, saying,

"I will trouble the waters as I lead"

Write	Hebrew *kathab* derived from the living letters Khaf, Chet, Beyt. Eber describes his friends, saying,

"from my hand of life into the secret place"

the vision,	Hebrew *chazown* derived from the living letters Chet, Zayin, Vav, Nun. Eber describes his friends, saying,

"as time joyfully aligns itself with Heaven and earth for the glorious inheritance"

and make it plain	Hebrew *ba'ar,* derived from the living letters Beyt, Aleph, Resh. Eber describes his friends, saying,

"from the speaking place I will be specific to lead"

upon tables,	Hebrew *luwach,* derived from the living letters Lamed, Tav, Chet. Eber describes his friends, saying,

"and I reveal the finishing from the beginning"

that he may run	Hebrew ruwts, derived from the living letters Resh, Vav, Tsade. Eber describes his friends saying,

"to look around the corner and recover our seats"

that readeth it.	Hebrew *qara'*, derived from the living letters Quph, Resh, Aleph. Eber describes his friends, saying,

"I look to reconnect the beginning of glory to its original strength."

Verse 3

For the vision	Hebrew *chazown*, derived from the living letters Chet, Zayin, Vav, Nun. Eber describes his friends, saying,

"As time joyfully aligns itself with Heaven and earth for the glorious inheritance,"

is yet for an appointed time,	Hebrew *mow'ed*, derived from the living letters Mem, Vav, Ayin, Dalet. Eber describes his friends, saying,

"The vibration of the deep waters connect our words to us from the fountain and through the door."

but at the end	Hebrew *qets*, derived from the living letters Quph, Tsade. Eber describes his friends, saying,

"My day of blessing has come as we humbly identify a completion."

it shall speak,	Hebrew *puwach,* derived from the living letters Pey, Vav, Chet. Eber describes his friends, saying,

"I speak of things seen and unseen of the everlasting"

and not lie:	Hebrew *kazab,* derived from the living letters Khaf, Zayin, Beyt. Eber describes his friends, saying,

"clean hands holding onto the seat as Christ within the speaking place"

though it tarry	Hebrew *mahahh,* derived from the living letters Mem, Hey, Hey. Eber describes his friends, saying,

"as the depths speak and breathe in and out and in and out"

wait for it	Hebrew *chakah,* derived from the living letters Chet, Khaf, Hey. Eber describes his friends, saying,

"as time is held in our hands we breath into the path of life"

because it will surely	Hebrew bow', derived from the living letters Beyt, Vav, Aleph. Eber describes his friends, saying,

"founded on a firm foundation and is connected to the path to ascend and descend though it is silent as it travels"

come,	Hebrew bow', derived from the living letters Beyt, Vav, Aleph. Eber describes his friends, saying,

"in its throne room releasing a sound from the strong leader"

it will not tarry.	Hebrew 'achar, derived from the living letters Aleph, Chet, Resh. Eber describes his friends, saying,

"leading in and out of his fullness of strength joyfully leading through unclaimed dimensions unto fulfillment."

Now I will combine this interpretation for somewhat easier reading. Mysteries are within what you are about to read, and they are meant to be read from within The Seven Spirits of the Lord. Be alert and open. Try not to make the interpretation fit your education from Babylon and religion. (*Note: The following is not edited. It is left as-is due to the Eber translation.*)

I will understand the importance to see from the portal from within the depths of my inheritance and the paths of the dimensions I will perceive. I am reminded to hold on to what my supply is from the original intent so that I may finish. Seated within righteousness safe and secure, I am well established in my mobile throne as I join my original intent within the path of righteousness and from this speaking place I will breathe as upon a window pane. I will look within time lowing the frequency of Heaven and I breathe into existence the portal that Heaven prepares to speak knowledge of secret places. I embrace the opportunity to ascend and descend from my speaking place as I finish the spoken acceptable word, I receive within my hand the everlasting breath that never ceases, and I am the breath of life that connects and joins the living. I am the portal that stands tall to breathe my word. I will trouble the waters as I lead from my hand of life in the secret place. As time joyfully aligns itself with Heaven and earth for the glorious inheritance from the speaking place I will be specific to lead as I reveal the finishing from the beginning. I look around corners and recover our seats, I look to reconnect the beginning of glory to its original strength. As time joyfully aligns itself with Heaven and earth for the glorious inheritance that the vibration of the deep waters connecting our words to us from the foundation and through the door. My day of blessing has come as we humbly identify a completion. I speak of things seen and unseen of the everlasting. Clean hands holding onto the seat as Christ within the speaking place as the depths speak and breathe in and out and in and out. As time is held in our hand we breathe the path of life founded on a firm foundation and it is connected to the path to ascend and descend though it is silent. I'm in my throne room releasing a sound from the strong leader leading in and out of His fullness of strength joyfully leading through unclaimed dimensions unto fulfillment.

Do you see the depths and width and height and timing of it differently now? It's the space-time continuum of Habakkuk 2:1–3. I encourage you now with this method of observation to determine if Choshek is only wicked and evil from Isaiah 5:20.

When the living letters speak as with the previous scripture in Habakkuk, I'm reminded that we are not only following in Yahshua's footsteps, but we are establishing a clear path for as many as Yahweh desires to follow. This path is no longer made difficult to find, as long as you are invited to find it. When Yahshua made his way into Jerusalem and eventually into the garden of Gethsemane, He began to ascend to a place called Golgotha, the place of the skull or death, a dark place. Was it Choshek? Once He was finished there, He descended into Hell and Death. Once in Hell and Death, He presented keys that unlocked the place of the end. Choshek was no longer a place of the abyss of death and separation. Yahshua presented the keys of the Kingdom in which I believe are judgment and justice in this case, and then he did the unthinkable. He crossed the great gulf that was fixed in place. It was uncrossable, but He had not only the keys out of Hell and Death, but the key to cross the great gulf.

Choshek was the path to freedom for those held captive in paradise. Paradise was incomplete in that the Messiah had not yet come and no man can ascend to the Father without the leading of the Messiah. Once Yahshua had reached paradise, He undoubtedly was greatly received by the saints of ancient times. Can you imagine when Adam, Eve, Abraham, Sarah, Isaac, Jacob, Moses, Aaron, Ruth, David, Daniel, Ezekiel, Joel and many others of ancient paths and times saw the portal open from the gulf? He preached to those in captivity and led them out of captivity into the presence of Yahweh. He presented them back unto the Father as a fulfilled word. This is now what we are called to do. We are called to ascend and descend into Choshek, the place of darkness, to find treasure that is looking for us to guide it back through the path of Yahshua and present it redeemed and fulfilled. As Yahshua said, *"I am the way, the truth, and the life: no man cometh unto the Father, but by me"* (John 14:6).

Darkness, the Universe, and Science

Have you ever heard of dark matter or dark energy? Before we describe what science thinks about it, let us look at some amazing numbers.

- *What is the size of our universe?*

  "The proper distance—the distance as would be measured at a specific time, including the present—between Earth and the edge of the observable universe is 46 billion light-years, making that diameter of the observable universe about 91 billion light-years."[41]

- *What is a light year?*

  It is the distance that light travels in a vacuum in one year. Light travels at 186,282 miles per second. One year has 31,536,000 seconds. That is thirty one million, five hundred and thirty-six thousand seconds. 5.87459e12, or 5 trillion, 874 billion, 590

---

41 "Universe." Wikipedia. Accessed August 24, 2018. https://en.wikipedia.org/wiki/Universe#Size_and_regions. "See also Nola Taylor Redd, "How Big Is the Universe?" Space.com. June 07, 2017. https://www.space.com/24073-how-big-is-the-universe.html.

million miles is how far light can travel in a vacuum, like space, in one year.[42]

- *How many stars are in the Milky Way galaxy?*

  There is no clear answer, but the very rough estimate is somewhere between 100 to 400 billion stars in just our galaxy.[43]

- *How many planets are in our galaxy?*

  At least 100 billion.[44]

- *How many galaxies are in our universe?*

  2 trillion.

- *What is dark matter and how much of it makes up our universe?*

  "Dark matter, unlike normal matter, does not interact with the electromagnetic force. This means it does not absorb, reflect or emit light, making it extremely hard to spot. In fact, researchers have been able to infer the existence of dark matter only from the gravitational effect it seems to have on visible matter. Dark matter seems to outweigh visible matter roughly six to one, making up about 27% of the universe. Here's a sobering fact: The matter we know and that makes up all stars and galaxies only accounts for 5% of the content of the universe! But what is dark matter? One idea is that it could contain 'supersymmetric particles' – hypothesized

---

42 See for example, "What Is a Light-Year?" NASA SpacePlace. May 23, 2018. Accessed March 27, 2019. https://spaceplace.nasa.gov/light-year/en/.
43 Elizabeth Howell. "How Many Stars Are in the Milky Way?" Space.com. March 30, 2018. https://www.space.com/25959-how-many-stars-are-in-the-milky-way.html.
44 "100 Billion Alien Planets Fill Our Milky Way Galaxy: Study." Space.com. January 02, 2013. https://www.space.com/19103-milky-way-100-billion-planets.html.

particles that are partners to those already known in the Standard Model. Experiments at the Large Hadron Collider (LHC) may provide more direct clues about dark matter."[45]

- ***What is dark energy and how much of it makes up our universe?***

  According to CERN, "Dark energy makes up approximately 68% of the universe and appears to be associated with the vacuum in space. It is distributed evenly throughout the universe, not only in space but also in time – in other words, its effect is not diluted as the universe expands. The even distribution means that dark energy does not have any local gravitational effects, but rather a global effect on the universe as a whole. This leads to a repulsive force, which tends to accelerate the expansion of the universe. The rate of expansion and its acceleration can be measured by observations based on the Hubble law. These measurements, together with other scientific data, have confirmed the existence of dark energy and provide an estimate of just how much of this mysterious substance exists."[46]

Scientists have admitted that they may only understand about one billionth of the universe. Scientist still debate the actual shape of the universe.[47] Scientists believe that there are only four forces at work naturally in the universe:

45 "Dark Matter." CERN Accelerating Science. Accessed Aug 24, 2018. https://home. cern/about/physics/dark-matter
46 *Ibid.*
47 Vanessa Janek. "What Shape Is the Universe?" Phys.org - News and Articles on Science and Technology. March 12, 2015. https://phys.org/news/2015-05-universe.html.

electromagnetism, gravity, and the strong and weak nuclear forces.[48] The universe is primarily made up of one element, hydrogen. Hydrogen makes up about 75% of the universe.[49]

Our minds, influenced by the slavery of Babylon, can be totally overwhelmed by the facts listed above. However, the mind of Christ—which we are to operate from—is not overwhelmed by these scientific theories and facts. The mind of Christ draws upon the assistance of everything that Yahweh has provided for us in this great age. We have been provided with the Seven Spirits of the Lord, the Seven Thunders, the Ancient Ones, the Desert Fathers and Mothers, the cloud of witnesses, and our personally assigned angels along with the angelic host. This is only what we know of that is available to us now. All of this has been given to us in order that we might not only understand but reveal its truth and glory to all creation.

26 Even the mystery which hath been hid from ages and from generations, but now is made manifest to his saints: 27 To whom God would make known what is the riches of the glory of this mystery among the Gentiles; which is Christ in you, the hope of glory… (Col. 1:26–27)

14 For as many as are led by the Spirit of God, they are the sons of God. 15 For ye have not received the spirit of bondage again to fear; but ye have received the Spirit of adoption, whereby we cry, Abba, Father. 16 The Spirit itself beareth witness with our spirit, that we are the children of God: 17 And if children, then heirs; heirs of God, and

48   Sam Kneller. "The Forces Holding the Universe Together." The Explanation. August 25, 2018. https://theexplanation.com/forces-holding-universe-together/.
49   "Hydrogen and Helium." StarDate. Accessed March 27, 2019. https://stardate.org/astro-guide/hydrogen-and-helium.

joint-heirs with Christ; if so be that we suffer with him, that we may be also glorified together. [18] *For I reckon that the sufferings of this present time are not worthy to be compared with the glory which shall be revealed in us.* [19] *For the earnest expectation of the creature waiteth for the manifestation of the sons of God.* [20] *For the creature was made subject to vanity, not willingly, but by reason of him who hath subjected the same in hope,* [21] *Because the creature itself also shall be delivered from the bondage of corruption into the glorious liberty of the children of God.* [22] *For we know that the whole creation groaneth and travaileth in pain together until now.* (Rom. 8:14–22)

Access Through Encounters

I am grateful for this amazing place of Up Here in Zion. Since we entered the ages of peace in 2009, we have been given invitations to new dimensions. Opportunities reside in these dimensions through encounters with all Heaven has to offer.

Some time ago I received an invitation for visitations from Enoch. He is the time-keeper as I've heard my friends say. In May of 2016, I was traveling from Panama City, Florida back to my home in Mobile, Alabama. Ian Clayton was with me, along with my son-in-law Trey, and a young man named Robert whom Ian was mentoring. We had been talking about *chayei olam*, life everlasting, when we decided to stop for dinner. As we entered the restaurant, the host prepared to seat us and asked if there were five of us. I started to say "No, only four," when suddenly Ian stopped me and said, "Yes, there are five of us." I was perplexed. Ian smiled and said, "I'll explain in a few."

The host seated us at a table for five. Four of the seats faced each other and the fifth was on the end. Ian and I sat across from each other as did the other two men. The chair on the end appeared to be empty until after we were seated when Ian nodded in recognition that the seat was occupied. For some reason, I whispered to Ian instead of speaking out loud, "Who is seated there?"

He smiled and said, "Enoch." Ian explained that it is courteous to nod in recognition, so we did. Our conversation about everlasting life had intrigued Enoch, Ian said, so he joined us to listen. I asked why. Ian said, "Enoch is the time-keeper that relates to *chayei olam*, life everlasting." It was an amazing experience that has since helped me in my private encounters and brought light to the following scriptures.

> *For the earth shall be filled with the knowledge of the glory of the Lord, as the waters cover the sea.* (Hab. 2:14)

> [19] *For [even the whole] creation [all nature] waits eagerly for the children of God to be revealed.* [20] *For the creation was subjected to frustration and futility, not willingly [because of some intentional fault on its part], but by the will of Him who subjected it, in hope* [21] *that the creation itself will also be freed from its bondage to decay [and gain entrance] into the glorious freedom of the children of God.* (Rom. 8:19–21 AMP)

I will share my view of what redeemed dark matter and dark energy in their glorious state will look and sound like in Part 2. Much treasure within our own world is yet to be discovered, but I believe the paths may first lead us away in to the depths of Choshek. Treasures await us there and I'm convinced that we are called to find them. That treasure is the Word of Yahweh, and we have the ability, as the family, of finding it and redeeming it back unto our Father. The church of the last ages has never fully awakened to this fact. It taught us to mind our own business: but my business *is* my Father's business. I am persuaded that this is pleasing to almighty Yahweh. I've heard people say things like, "It all belongs to the Lord." If that is true in their lives, then have they been good stewards of the gift of handling His business? But, truthfully, there hasn't been a knowledge of what to do with what Yahweh has given. This way of thinking has produced a church stuck within a cycle of helplessness and very little results. The church has not had the heart for redemption nor the understanding of it. I hear some saying now, "Redemption of what?" It's the redemption of His Word. We are still on this earth to fulfill His word. There are many great stories of redemption that many have witnessed—including me. But my question is why stop at where we have been? We have been called to do the greater things so let us go where no man has gone. Yahshua has declared it and has challenged us to follow His path.

The Tallit as a Path to Choshek

In the spring of 2017, I had the honor and pleasure to visit with Grant and Samantha Mahoney at their home in New Zealand. While visiting, many great things effected my life, but one particular thing that Grant did allowed me to better engage within this great age of peace that yields everlasting revelation.

I had been rather suddenly drawn to the tallit, the Hebrew prayer shawl with its ancient origins. I had been privately inquiring in my heart about it since I had noticed Ian Clayton using one in worship and draping one over his pulpit before ministering. I had seen tallits used during the war ages. Although I thought they were cool-looking, at that time it didn't strike me as something I needed. When Ian began to engage with the tallit, I was struck by it and was drawn to it. I didn't have the understanding at the time, but I knew something was about to happen.

One day while in Grant and Sam's home, Grant said he had a very special gift for me. It was morning and I was sitting at their dining table. Ian was visiting too. We were chatting when Grant came into the room with a little square black bag. Ian said, "Oh wow!" He knew it was Grant's personal tallit. Grant took it out of the bag, unfolded it, and handed it to me. He said Yahweh had asked him to give it to me.

I didn't even know what to do. I was overwhelmed, and besides that, I didn't have any knowledge of how to handle a tallit. Ian described the purpose of the four corners and the knots known as the tzitzit that represent blessings. Grant and Ian robed me with the tallit, and when they did, I immediately went somewhere. That somewhere was into Mount Zion and within the cloud of glory. I was given a path to the portal gates of Ayin that spirals through Ghah to the night skies of Choshek.

If you are unfamiliar with the tallit or how to engage with it, do not be dismayed. It is a personal matter, but it is good to know some of the procedure. Positioned on the front of many tallits is a blessing written in Hebrew. Most declare the following blessing:

> Blessed are You, Lord our God (Yahweh), King of the universe, who has sanctified us with His commandments (word), and commanded us to wrap ourselves in Tzitzit (promised blessings).

Traditionally, after declaring the blessing written on the tallit but before you cover yourself, you kiss the written blessing. This is not necessary, but it is Jewish tradition. There are many references you can Google for the procedure of robing yourself with the tallit. I usually completely cover myself and grab either the tzitzit of the back two corners or at times all four corners. Once I have finished with my time totally covered, I will bring the tallit to my shoulders until I am finished. It is amazing!

I believe using the tallit is one of the ways to find the path in and out of Choshek. Engaging under the tallit is not the only way, for you can go into Choshek whenever and wherever you need to and whenever you are called to. What a great thing for us to be able to say, for that was not the case until the ages changed in 2009. Let us who hear this sound never take it for granted. If you have Ruach Kodesh, the Holy Ghost, residing in you, then let your mind be at peace, for He is a gift sent from Yahshua to guide us and He knows what we need. Often Holy Ghost compels me to cover myself under the tallit in honor so that I can better hear and see. I am thankful for that, and I love it.

* * *

Yahweh loves the world and all of His creation. As it says in John 3:16, *"For God so loved the world, that he gave his only begotten Son, that whosoever believeth in him should not perish, but have everlasting life."* I believe without a doubt that we are His best treasure. We are considered precious in worth and value, for we are family. I desire to be about my Father's business, so I pursue that with all of my heart. When the lost who are looking to find their way see the light of our Father and creator in us, then He will draw all men unto Himself. We who call them home to this great place of liberty will reveal all treasure held captive in darkness, and all shall be found.

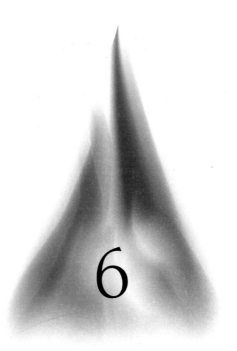

6

THE PROGRESSIVE THRONE ROOMS

Think of a throne room. What image comes to mind? I automatically picture an ornate, majestic gold seat that stands alone on an elaborately designed platform draped in royal colors. I'm sure I've been influenced by pictures of genuine throne rooms. No doubt, I'm influenced by movies, too. I think of the movies about Queen Elizabeth and the many throne rooms shown. I've Googled throne rooms and the ones I have pulled up all have similarities: ornate seats, extravagant surroundings. Since I've been engaged in the Ages of Peace, my perspectives about throne rooms have greatly changed.

First and foremost, a throne room represents and exudes authority. Authority is established by trust and great respect. Righteous authority is founded in love and is seated in mercy and peace. This kind of authority is honored and revered, for it upholds the laws that establish and declare judgment for justice's sake. A throne room established on righteous authority releases and receives communication from anyone who is joined to and protected by the throned one. It also renders judgment on lawlessness and rebellion so that the standard of righteousness, peace, and joy may continue to stand. This is possible because of the establishment of honor and the integrity and character of the authority of the one seated in such a great place. As long as the authority has power to exercise judgment for justice's sake, then the throne is an awesome place of protection and provision. If respect has ceased to flow from or to the throne, then the throne room is just a room with a fancy chair in it. Without respect and honor, it represents loss and nothingness to a woeful, lawless society. But with respect and honor established upon the foundation of Yahweh's love, His Throne Room is eternally a place of everlasting peace.

School Day Lesson in Honor

In 1971, life was very different than it is now. I was thirteen then, and racial integration was in full swing in the southern states of the United States. Our nation was in the throes of a political war (Vietnam) that could not be won. Although we were affected by the turmoil of that day, you could still find honesty. Not only my life, but our nation and the world were affected by the war.

North Brewton Junior High School was a small country school in Alabama. When I entered the seventh grade there, my classmates and I were introduced to our first African-American teacher. Mrs. Spears quickly became one of my favorite teachers. She was a great teacher, but also one of the nicest and sweetest ladies I knew. In some ways, she reminded me of my precious grandmother. We all loved her.

After school had been in session for about a month, my friends and I started to do what junior high boys sometimes do. We thought everything was funny and began to pick on each other in Mrs. Spears' class. We were disruptive. She would correct us, and we would apologize. Then, not much later, we would disrupt class again. This cycle went on for a couple of days one week. We weren't belligerent rebels; we were giggly boys thumping each other or throwing paper at each other whenever Mrs. Spears would turn her back to write on the chalkboard. She would hear us laughing and would correct us again. We would say, "Yes, ma'am." But soon we were up to the same pattern again. There were five of us and we didn't mean to upset her. We just couldn't help ourselves.

Finally one day, sweet Mrs. Spears was tired of the continued disruptions. She gave us a firm warning in her gentle way. She said, "Now boys, you know I care about you and I want you to learn, but if you continue to misbehave then you are not only hurting yourselves, but others can't learn either." We apologized to her and the class. She thanked us and proceeded to give us a warning. She said that this day was a different day and she had made a decision that she would not tolerate the unruliness any longer. She said there would be no more warnings and no turning back.

We did good for a short while. But, quoting from *Forrest Gump*, "Stupid is as stupid does." We started our little laughs. Mrs. Spears turned ever so gently and told the class that she would be right back. We thought she had gone to the restroom, so we had a good ol' time.

Suddenly over the intercom came a voice that scared us out of our minds. It was the voice of Mr. Page. THE PRINCIPAL! He was a true man in charge who demanded respect and order. He had a great smile and we loved his approval, but his angry look was one of a kind. His firm voice was distinct as he said, "The following unruly boys are to come to my office immediately... Aaron Smith, Lamar Wilson, William Holland, Darrell McCall and Dennis Jackson." Everyone in the class gave a big sigh of "Ohhh, nooo...," except those of us who were doomed. Silently, in fear and trembling, we proceeded to the office.

While walking nervously to the office, we started blaming each other for our pending demise. Except for Lamar, who was always the tough guy—he said, "I'm not scared."

As we entered Mr. Page's small office, we looked around to see if we could spot the mysterious, rumored electric paddle. Of course, there never was one, but we later claimed we might have seen it in his closet. He didn't need an electric one. The paddle he had was powerful enough.

Mrs. Spears was in the office already. Mr. Page asked her, "Are these the boys?"

With tears in her eyes, she answered, "Yes."

Mr. Page told us to apologize. Afterwards, he respectfully told Mrs. Spears that this wouldn't happen again. He told her how much he appreciated her teaching. He let her know he would tell our parents of the disruption, and he knew they would give her their full support.

She said, "I love the boys. I just want them to do well in school."

We felt horrible. Mr. Page made us wait for a few minutes

in his office. We thought we were out of the woods.

No. He was waiting for break time when most of the school would be around to witness our punishment. He pulled us out into the front entrance foyer for all to see. He told those witnessing what had happened and that it was payday. Our school had about 300 students and most of them were present. Mr. Page asked with a strong authoritative voice, "Who wants to go first?"

Tough guy Lamar answered with a slight hint of defiance, "I'll go first!"

Mr. Page said, "Step right up, bend over, and hold on to your knees."

The first lick sounded like a high-powered rifle going off. Lamar's feet slightly came off the ground. Lamar turned to look at us. His eyes and face were like those of a cat in sheer terror. Two more licks followed. Tears began to stream down tough guy's face.

Mr. Page asked with great resolve, "Who would like to go next?"

I quickly jumped in. I didn't want to witness that again knowing it was coming to me. When the first lick landed I realized why tough man wasn't so tough anymore. It was a pain on my butt I'd never felt before. I was really glad there were only three licks. A fourth could've been embarrassing.

Mrs. Spears was present. She stood to the side. Tears flowed down her face, and she was quietly saying, "I'm sorry." Total silence hung over the crowd as they witnessed the consequences of what happens when you are continually disrespectful toward authority.

From that day on, we took care of Mrs. Spears. In the

mornings, we stood in the parking lot, waiting for her to arrive, so we could carry her books in to the classroom. She was uncomfortable with it, but we insisted. It was from our hearts. We cleaned the chalkboard and would do whatever it took to honor our beloved Mrs. Spears. Our parents were embarrassed and apologized to Mr. Page and Mrs. Spears at the next parent/teacher meeting.

That day of reckoning was one of the best things that had ever happened to all five of us. Thank you, Mrs. Spears and Mr. Page. That was 43 years ago and I often still think of that horrifying experience which helped shape my life in learning to respect authority.

* * *

Many reading this probably think we received cruel and unnecessary punishment. Corporal punishment practices have stopped in schools due to abuse, and I understand the position many take against it. But, it was a different day then. I don't know about anywhere else, but in my community and school, we knew each other. There was a code of honor and respect for authority that was set in stone. Everyone I knew lived by that code, and we thought everyone else did, too. We had proper, peaceful authority in place. We respected and served those who had authority. When lawlessness began to creep in, and at times it did, it was first closely examined to determine the motive, and then it was dealt with in a swift and sure manner.

When the media began to fuel lawlessness and corruption, codes of honor and respect began to unravel. If something like what happened to us five boys happened today, it would go viral. Someone would video it from their phone, post it, and call it cruel and unusual punishment. Mr. Page would lose his job, be cast out of the education system, and probably wind up in court. People might even march against our school to shut it down or play the blame game, maybe even making us into victims. But dignity, which is the state or quality of being worthy of honor or respect, was important to us then. The word *dignity* is rarely used anymore, but even if it is used it has become something cheap and worthless from the spheres of lawless influence.

All of man's earthly authority is in jeopardy in a society that has no respect for the principles of life and especially the Kingdom. Remember that all authority is given by Yahweh, for He is the only authority. If you see corrupt authority, then know Yahweh has lifted His grace off that land. It is usually due to the hearts of man in that place. Their hearts have turned away from a loving God to care only for themselves. Love has left the building, and that land will become a desolate place.

My Initial Throne Room Encounters

I know now that I heard my first voice from the Throne Room in 1974. When I was later awakened to the Throne Room in the late 1970s, I couldn't see it. I could only sense it. In 1984, I was working in New Orleans, and one Saturday Robbie and I took our two-year-old daughter, Jessica, to the New Orleans Zoo. It was a marked day which I'll never forget. On that pleasant day we were walking around the different sites of the zoo when we made a turn through the beautiful, majestic live oaks to see the outdoor seal pool, which is surrounded by huge pillars placed in an oval pattern. I didn't see the seal pool. Instead, I heard sounds from dimensions that I had not awakened to yet. I recognized them within my spirit, but my spirit mind was in a fog for I was just beginning to engage this dimension. I was being hovered over in the spirit: everything lit up, the pillars came alive, and the entire place was suspended in space with all of creation at its attention.

I heard Yahweh say, "This is Our Throne Room."

All I could say was, "Wow!"

It is difficult to describe, but in that encounter, my path had become clearer. My taste for the dimensions was like that of a child tasting real food for the first time. Not much was happening dimensionally in those days. The faith movement was in full swing, and for that I'm grateful. It assisted me in many ways. While it was not the end of my path, it was a great help on my journey. Many things that worked for those that were of that movement wouldn't seem to work for me. If they had, I might have never found this great place.

In the Fall of 1987, I was new on the church staff under Apostle F. Nolan Ball at The Rock of Panama City, Florida. I had served as youth pastor for two years at a church in Millbrook, Alabama. My life as a youth pastor was lively, and Robbie and I loved it. After five years serving as youth pastor in these two locations, I had pastored over five hundred teens. In the years following, I was honored to be called on to do many of their weddings. I performed nearly one hundred weddings.

During my time in Panama City, I encountered the Throne Room again. This time it was dimensionally by the spirit. What I mean by that is that I was not just seeing it in 3D. I tried to explain to others what I was seeing, but was unable to due to the limited language I had to describe it then. Now I know what I encountered was like a tesseract using the fourth dimension of space and time. All I could say in those days was that I saw thrones and throne rooms that faced into the Throne Room in the center, but there was no back side to the rooms. They could only be dimensionally discerned from a tesseract-like model of inside out and outside in. I also could not explain that each throne room wasn't any farther away or closer than the others. I knew their unusual, moving, indeterminate placement had to do with our equality and the strength of that equality within the Kingdom. This vision was given to me to better understand the fullness of John 17 of us being one within each other.

When Yahweh revealed the four wheels of Ezekiel to me, I saw the Throne Room again. I believe that Ezekiel chapters 1 and 10 and Revelation 4 all describe the Throne Room. All three speak of different positions and purposes. Although they all have similarities and agree in purpose, some of the details change in a type of progression. First, their purpose is to describe the greatness of the I AM and His speaking place. All the fantastic things and beings described have duties which reveal the happenings in and from the speaking place. The accounts from Ezekiel and John of the Throne Room of Yahweh describe the living glory of Yahweh made manifest. The descriptions from both writers are mysterious. They seem to be heavily coded, making understanding appear unattainable. Not so! I am fully convinced that Yahweh desires for us to discern and know everything about this great place. But it cannot be discerned by even the best minds and theologians. It is only spiritually discerned by invitation.

I now want to do a simple description of my view of some of the symbolism of these three incredible depictions of the progressive throne rooms. I believe they describe not only Yahweh's abode, but they also describe us—those who have engaged our glory and thrones of glory within Him.

First Throne Room: Ezekiel

Let us start by looking into the symbolism of the first throne room found in Ezekiel chapter 1:4–14. As Eber reveals the hidden meanings behind the obscure descriptions of the throne room and its activities, I will translate with my view and thoughts.

Ezekiel 1:4–14

> *⁴ And I looked, and, behold, a whirlwind came out of the north, a great cloud, and a fire infolding itself, and a brightness was about it, and out of the midst thereof as the colour of amber, out of the midst of the fire.*
>
> *⁵ Also out of the midst thereof came the likeness of four living creatures. And this was their appearance; they had the likeness of a man.*
>
> *⁶ And every one had four faces, and every one had four wings.*
>
> *⁷ And their feet were straight feet; and the sole of their feet was like the sole of a calf's foot: and they sparkled like the colour of burnished brass.*
>
> *⁸ And they had the hands of a man under their wings*

on their four sides; and they four had their faces and their wings.

⁹ Their wings were joined one to another; they turned not when they went; they went every one straight forward.

¹⁰ As for the likeness of their faces, they four had the face of a man, and the face of a lion, on the right side: and they four had the face of an ox on the left side; they four also had the face of an eagle.

¹¹ Thus were their faces: and their wings were stretched upward; two wings of every one were joined one to another, and two covered their bodies.

¹² And they went every one straight forward: whither the

spirit was to go, they went; and they turned not when they went.

¹³ As for the likeness of the living creatures, their appearance was like burning coals of fire, and like the appearance of lamps: it went up and down among the living creatures; and the fire was bright, and out of the fire went forth lightning.

¹⁴ And the living creatures ran and returned as the appearance of a flash of lightning.

Verse 4 describes a whirlwind out of the north, a great cloud and a fire enfolding itself.

- Whirlwinds represent a connection of a Heaven and earth change. They can represent the clearing out of a path. The whirlwind here, coming out of the north, represents coming out of the hidden place. It depicts an earthly deposit made from Choshek, the place of the hidden treasures.

- *A great cloud* could be the great cloud of witnesses who are within Yahweh. They are part of the legal process in Heaven for the fulfillment of the rights to treasure returning to its original intent.

- The *fire infolding itself* is the tesseract of our throne rooms and how they appear as Yahweh's glory is revealed in us. (How awesome is that?!)

Verse 5 introduces the four living creatures coming out of the fire and describes their appearance as like man.

- The number *four* refers to the four corners and therefore speaks of a three dimensional space, be it Heaven or earth.

- When the creatures come out of the fire, it reveals us coming from within Yahweh and Yahweh in us as man—much like the appearance of a tesseract.

- As their appearance was like *man*, it validates for us that they are expressions of us and dimensionally are us. These are the light beings of us. (Cool, huh?!)

- Note: the creatures were *living*. They were expressing life from the Father. It is important to see these creatures not as monsters, but as extensions of our expressions of life within Yahweh being revealed.

Verse 6 describes a few of the characteristics of the living creatures; specifically, each has four faces and four wings.

- When Yahweh began to teach me how He desires me to recognize the living numbers, He showed me how they connect and interchange. To me, the four faces represent the four corners of each direction. It's as if the north, south, east, and west each have four corners within themselves. These numbers add up to 16, in which is not only the witness of eight, but it also points to the finished work of this age of peace. The ages usually are made up of 7s. When they mirror each other, they continue to count: *8, 9, 10, 11, 12, 13, 14,* instead of beginning at 1–7 again. Each stage of the 7s has a witness representative of 1. The additional two 1s brings us to 16. Therefore, 16 is made up of two groups of 7s and the 2 witnesses. But in relation to Eber, the number 16 correlates with the living letter *Ayin*. Ayin is the portal to and from Choshek. (Wow!)

- The four wings of the living creatures likewise represent the same numbers as the four faces, but the wings add movement and the ability to change dimensions. They can change to any dimension of any direction within the dimensions of earth or

Heaven. In Revelation 4, we encounter the creatures with six wings. To me, this speaks of spiritual quantum entanglement operating within not only the four corners but beyond the four corners into dimensions that continually change position. This speaks of all creation, including all universes and depths of Heaven. Nothing is hidden anywhere. (Amazing!)

Verse 7 describes the feet of the four living creatures.

- Eber reveals a hidden message of the path that the living creatures travel upon.

- The mystery of their feet, due to their burnished brass, golden color, uncovers the fact that they represent royalty. The living creatures are royal. They are bringing the supply of Heaven, be it large or small, down one straight path through any size portal. This is the mystery of the hooves of a calf: they are small but designed to uphold weight or glory.

Verse 8 describes the mysterious physical build of the creatures.

- The hidden secret of the *hand* is revealed through Eber. The hand here represents the ability to hold onto the doorpost of eternity.

- The *man* represents, from Eber's revelation, the strength to carry the burden of a word and take it to the place for it to resonate on the sea of glass.

- The description of the hands of a man *under their wings* does not naturally fit or have a typical function in this position on any natural body. Eber reveals the paradox of a wing and a hand ascending and descending together within a dimensional shift. It's the hand of God within the hand of man that is well able to carry the burden of righteousness and its voice into multi-dimensions.

- *On their four* are the four Hebrew letters Aleph, Resh, Beyt, Ayin. *On* is represented as "on earth" and *four* refers to the four winds on the earth. The winds are committed to the ancient paths, not paths newly made by man.

- *Sides* is represented in Hebrew by Resh, Beyt and Ayin. Eber says the depths of the signs from the ancient portal will speak from all sides about hidden things from beginning to finishing.

- The unusual description *and they four* is interpreted through our friend Eber. The letters of Aleph, Resh, Beyt and Ayin describe that all four are in on the responsibility of carrying the burden and connecting what was promised from the beginning which will find its way through the portal.

- As we continue to engage with the description of the living creatures, we see their faces described from the mysteries of the living letters. The four letters that reveal what *had their faces* really mean are Pey, Nun, Yod and Mem. This literally means "to speak from righteousness by beginning and finishing from the creative waters." That very last part of the creative waters is speaking of the sea of glass and the sound that comes from the faces.

- The conclusion of this verse, *and their wings,* finishes, from the perspective of Eber, with a resounding proclamation of the position of standing in the precise dimension to speak.

Verse 9 describes the position of their wings along with the direction that they were to go.

- The first words of the verse repeat how the last verse finished—*Their wings*—but I see it differently here. The wings are positioned to stand to speak. Eber reveals that the wings were joined one to another to depict the rehearsal of this new beginning within the house and to lead by the everlasting example. The living letters express much more than is translated into English. It is a sharing of the crown and releasing breath in unison. The revealing from the living letters of the reference to another is astounding. It literally means "I will laugh as we connect Heaven and earth to a finished work." That seems bizarre until we begin to see the big picture.

- The mysterious description of how they stayed on a straight path doesn't reveal why. It is stated plainly that they do not turn. Here is something that is so hidden and very important. The living letters, once again, are ready to reveal why this is even mentioned. *They turned not* is not translated correctly into English. In Hebrew, the phrase was speaking of a path from within and without. *When they went* is defined in Hebrew as a spiraling bolt of lightning guided by the hand to release blessing. *They went* speaks of ascending and guiding the hand to the specific blessing point. The reference to *every one* speaks of the strong leader crowned mysteriously to and by the breath. I am amazed at the call of the mysteries to be discovered. They are like a kid who has been playing hide and seek for a very long time and are ready to be found. The Seven Thunders are assisting in this great find. *Straight* emphasizes entering the portal within the house that connects dimensions. Likewise the reference to *forward* speaks of the expression of righteousness that exudes from the heirs. The power of this righteousness traverses the universe vibrating the upper and lower waters.

Verse 10 describes the four faces of the creatures. Much of what is described in this verse is crucial in order to grasp the mysteries of the directions of our throne rooms. Our throne rooms are mobile and we must discern our path in order to rule righteously from within Zion.

Let us stop for a moment and honor the Spirit of Understanding.

Spirit of the Lord, we thank you for pointing us to The Spirit of Understanding for she is amazing in her ability to break down the pieces of the puzzle and the skill to know how to connect the dots. Spirit of Understanding, we engage with you and your frequency from the ancient paths.

As I engage with the heart of Eber to find the hidden depths of the living letters, I call upon any and all of the Seven Thunders to assist in revealing the heart of Yahweh in these amazing throne rooms.

- *As for the likeness* describes the position of standing at the portal of Heaven and earth to remember the frequencies of Heaven breathing in and out sounds and the light of the finish. *Of their faces* speaks that these sounds are of righteousness and have the ability to traverse anywhere through the frequencies of Heaven.

- *They four* speaks of going into Olam from the four corners from the house and through the portal. This not only speaks of eternal things but of everlasting things. The next reference to *had the face* speaks from the face that stands in the paths of everything that resonates from Heaven. The face is significant to not only confront but to direct one's attention to an intended goal or outcome.

- *Of a man* refers to one who is to lead from the door to sound out. The next phrase, *of the face,* refers to the strong leader revealing glory of discerning today and tomorrow throughout creation. Why a man face first in this first reference is that man must be the leader of the first mentioned throne room due to our likeness of the Godhead. This is different from the starting point in the second throne room of Ezekiel 10. Likewise in John's revelation in Revelation 4 the leader is again different than the first one in Ezekiel 10. The fourth throne room is a return to the man, but the man there looks and is very different from the first. This man is gloriously a light being in a tesseract and is symbolic of *chayei olam*.

- *Of a lion* is the point of retaining the memory of your position and governing all creation from the authority that is called righteousness.

- *On the right side* speaks the direction in which to carry the burden that connects the beginnings of and from the house and its portal to the hidden treasures.

- *And they four* speaks of the strength of all four corners to hold onto and carry the everlasting connections while seeing around corners. This speaks of discernment that connects all timelines or time dimensions.

- *Had the face* identifies holding on to the frequencies of the strong leader connecting to the understanding.

- *Of an ox:* positioned in right standing and crowned with the ability to carry the glory while ascending and descending.

- *On the left side:* engaging into the never ending supply that enables the strong leader to lead while moving up and down and to teach the ways of how to engage this never ending supply.

- *Four also had* reveals that the burden bearer governs the house by His eye.

- In the final living words and letters—Nun, Shin, Resh, נֶשֶׁר—of this great verse, we see the reference to *the face of an eagle.* The eagle is the finisher who ascends and descends through all dimensions. The eagle represents the heirs who are the awe-spark of this beginning throne room, but by the time we see the third throne room, the eagle is the flying eagle.

Verse 11 describes the joining of the creatures' faces and wings.

- *Their faces:* the mouth speaks righteousness while speaking all necessary frequencies.

- *and their wings:* ascending with a releasing of Heaven's heart and speaking it.

- *Stretched* references speaking and making sounds that can be heard around the corner from the door.

- *Upward:* looking within the upper waters for the perception of learning.

- *Two* is discerned by Eber as holding onto the witness of righteousness to connect the upper waters to the frequencies of the lower waters.

- *Of everyone* is the strong single leader connecting the crown.

- *Joined* is a new beginning in the house to the original intent.

- *One* is leading and connecting the royalty. It is the sharp and continuing life of dots connecting in the vast sea of mystery, waiting to be reconciled.

- *To another* is like holding on while spiraling within the breath.

- *And two*: the walking bodies that make their connection to the earth from within all creation through the breath.

- *Covered* refers to the wings that cover and support while releasing the breath of light. This breath of light is mysterious, but remember everything Yahweh creates has some type of breath, be it from oxygen or photonics reactions. The breath allows it to exude its glory to live.

- *Their bodies*: it aligns perfectly to the coverings in that their bodies are made up of Gimel, Vav, Yod, Hey which speak of carrying the treasures and connecting the treasures to the rightful heirs moving through all creation to breathe the light of His glory.

Verse 12 describes the moving of the creatures.

- *And they went* is to traverse the universe while finding the path to Yahweh's open hands.

- *Every one*: the strong leader of everyone is crowned.

- *Straight*: as above as it is below, so that the house is governed by the one head.

- *Forward* is our speaking place that continues to propagate life which sparks momentous transformation.

- *Whither the spirit* means to see around corners joining spirit and matter to open up chayei olam.

- *Was to go* refers to a path of ancient teachers that call forth to us for the blessing.

- *They went*: supporting and creating an ascending and descending house.

- *And they turned* refers to a shielding of the spiraling pathway from house to house or mountain to mountain.

- *Not when they went* again mysteriously reveals a very hidden message that is speaking of a regenerative power of the heart obtaining true knowledge and maintaining clean hands. This is a reference to Psalm 24.

Verse 13 describes the living creatures like burning coals of fire.

- *As for the likeness*: I am a door always listening for the supply from the never ending supply of Heaven for it is secured and marked for me.

- *Of the living creatures*: The living creatures live dimensionally inside out and outside in. They traverse the universe coding and rewriting all dark matter according to the scroll of Yahweh.

- *Their appearance*: The depths of mysterious seas are governed from the beginning origin by the strong leaders that are fully alive, looking and breathing His name.

- *Was like burning*: The foundation pours forth and connects all things hidden in mystery to be revealed through the leaders.

- *Coals*: Through the journey of dimensions an ascending and descending dance takes place through the leaders.

- *Of fire*: Exhibits the strength of the silent awe-spark of Yahweh that transports through portals and dimensions.

- *And like the appearance*: The never ending supply of Heaven from the beginning is governed by our breath and the strength of our hands that are clean and joined together to uphold any amount of glory.

- *Of lamps*: The light of the leader speaks words that create a transformation and opens doors.

- *It went up and down*: The breath we release is a divine light that leads those with clean hands in their ascending and descending.

- *Among the living creatures*: This is the tent wall traversing the universe in great confidence, strength and glorious release.

- *And the fire*: This speaks of the strength of the silent leader that lays hold of Yahweh's essence.

- *Was bright*: This is the son—the heir walks as a supplier and trader arcing divine light and breath with Melchizedek.

- *And out of the fire*: is the engaging sound that states that "I will lay hold."

- *Went forth*: refers to the action of traversing the cosmos as a king/priest in great strength.

- *Lightning*: is the resemblance of a house that leads in holiness.

Verse 14 describes the brilliance of the creatures' movements.

- This reference to *and the living creatures* describes from Eber the tent wall and its expansion. Look into the depths of the living letters and you will see what the living creatures are genuinely doing.

- *Ran* reveals the nature of the governor of righteousness who is a strong burden bearer.

- *And returned:* the Awe-Spark secures the house.

- *As the appearance* is the never ending supply governed by Melchizedek's breath of light.

- The very cool expression *of a flash of lightning* in Hebrew literally means *the house nourishes holiness and understanding through all dimensions.* Holiness is not a meek and lowly characteristic of Yahweh: it is a powerful bolt of lightning. In Alabama, we know what it is like to experience the power of a bolt of lightning. If you survive being near enough to one, you hear it, see it, feel it, and in some cases, smell it. I have been fortunate to survive a strike from as close as 30 feet away. It was deafening to the point of leaving behind a loud, ringing, high-pitched frequency. It is the brightest white light which can nearly blind you. The impact of a lightning bolt's Heaven and earth connection shakes everything in you and around you. The aroma after a close strike is amazing. The atmosphere smells so clean. This is Yahweh's awe-spark!

The Unfolding of the Second and Third Throne Rooms

Ezekiel chapter 10 in many ways looks and sounds the same as chapter 1, that is, at least in the functions of wheels and angels. A primary change in chapter 10 compared to chapter 1 is that one of the faces of the living creatures changes from an ox to a cherub. This, to me, represents a dimensional shift and position of the living creatures. In the reference to the Throne Room in Revelation 4, the same creature changes again. This time the face is that of a calf or, perhaps better interpreted, a sprout or shoot. Why the changes and why is it the same face that keeps changing? I inquired of the Seven Spirits of the Lord and they referenced the Seven Thunders. Ezekiel 1:10 reveals a pattern or process flow of faces. The first mentioned is the face of a man. The second is the face of a lion. This lion face is on the right side. The third, positioned off the left side, is the face of an ox. Then the fourth face is that of an eagle.

I believe the man-face is positioned in the east. This face primarily looks from the east. Although it can look in all four directions just as the other faces can, it comes from the east. The east speaks of the leader.

The face of the lion is on the right or north side. Judgment is released from the north. The roar of the lion is the sound of pending judgment. Scientists say that lions roar for two reasons. The first is to make all aware of their strength and greatness. After making a kill, the lion roars again to claim what is his or hers. The north aligned with the lion is perfect.

It is crucial to engage the Spirit of Understanding concerning the importance of the directions. The three different positions of the faces and their directions describe a dimensional ascending or descending. The number 3 usually indicates that Yahweh is building or has built something. His basic, natural design is built around the triangle. The three different accounts found in Ezekiel 1, 10 and Revelation 4 describe the throne rooms in three progressive states. I believe spiritually as we move into position and engage our scrolls written by Yahweh and not the scrolls of man and a curse, we will experience the three dimensional throne rooms. They are in progression from the primary marking points of the ox, then the cherub, and finally the calf or shoot found in Revelation chapter 4.

Figure 1: The Progressive Throne Rooms (Aaron Smith)

The Four Corners Arranged Through the Ages.

EZEKIEL 1:10

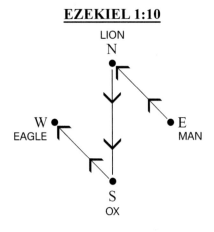

EZEKIEL 10:14

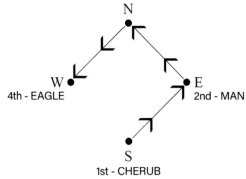

REVELATIONS 4:7

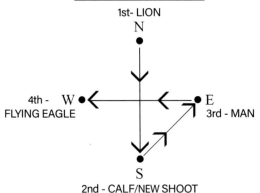

Figure 2: The Progressive Throne Rooms (Aaron Smith)

The Tesseract of the Fourth Dimension.

The Throne Room of Outside In and Inside Out.

All 6 directions from the West.

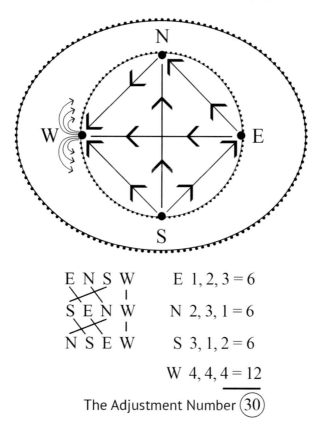

E N S W	E 1, 2, 3 = 6
S E N W	N 2, 3, 1 = 6
N S E W	S 3, 1, 2 = 6
	W 4, 4, 4 = 12

The Adjustment Number ⟨30⟩

- All signs point West.
- West (U.S.) is the epitome of Babylon.
- The eagle is the national bird.
- The flying eagle of Rev. 4 speaks of a dimensional shift.
- The finish will come from America.

Dimensional Paths of the Progressive Throne Rooms

I am grateful for the many sons and daughters who relate to me. Teresa Bowen, Elijah Ward, and Joey Dixon are three faithful seers and associates of mine who engage with the dimensions where our scrolls call us to witness and work from within. I've asked permission from each of them to reveal their views and perspectives of the throne rooms. They all share similarities and distinct differences in the dimensions they speak from.

Please note: you will hear more and more from these seers in the near future. Elijah Ward is one of the most dynamic, up and coming sounds out of our house at The Rock of Mobile. Joey Dixon is one of my relatives. He sees dimensionally as well as anyone I know. Every time Yahweh invites him into a new view, he never hesitates to engage. He gets so excited that I can see it on his face every time he sees something new. He is never jealous or afraid of what he discovers, but brings it to me immediately. Teresa Bowen is already well-received for her revelation and understanding of the Zadok priesthood. She also has a great understanding of the constellations in relation to their Heaven and earth connection. You will see that in her throne room perspective below. All three are very humbled in their findings. All true seers are that way, for they are not self-promoting: they are there for the cause. This heart-attitude moves the Father to honor them with much more, for they honor Him and His treasure.

Engage with and enjoy their throne room perspectives. Remember that you have your perspective, too. We all have similar surroundings and purposes, but our throne rooms are unique to us as individuals.

*   *   *

Elijah Ward's Perspective

Throne Room Mountain Revelation

This throne room is the mountain of Zion that has been revealed throughout history and prophesied about by ancients of our faith for thousands of years. It's the place He went away to, to prepare for me in John 14:3. Like the house of many mansions, where we have believed for so long, He has created a "room" for each of us. To me, this is the mountain of many mountains where I believe every single son of the Father's house and family is given a unique throne room mountain to be seated in and rule as kings in the earth. This mountain will inevitably bring the end of Babylonian rule or captivity in our lives. In Daniel 2, the stone which *"was cut out by no human hand"* (Dan. 2:34 ESV)[50] shattered the image of Babylon, ending its rulership, and it *"became a great mountain and filled the whole earth"* (Dan. 2:35 ESV). So, the establishment of this mountain is inseparably entangled with the event of the shattering of Babylon. Why is it important to engage and be seated in your mountain? Because the beginning of His mountain's establishment in your life is consequentially indicative of the end of Babylon's hold on your life. *Thank you, Yahweh! Take Your seat in this mountain.*

---

50 Compare this to Yahshua, the Living Stone, in 1 Peter 2:4.

Throne Room Mountain Encounter

As we transitioned into the age of Zion in August of 2017, instead of just talking about it, I began to see and encounter my throne room. I went into the cloud and saw a huge mountain, shadows on the side facing me as light came from behind it, as if the earthly sun was setting behind it. In the center of the mountain about halfway up was a stone doorway opening to enter into the mountain. From that stone doorway was coming different colors of light in the form of a rainbow—it was the Seven Spirits. Fascinated, I gazed at the mountain, and I felt drawn by the light of the Seven Spirits, as if they were inviting me in. So I began walking toward the mountain and ascending the hill. While ascending, I noticed the mountain was alive. It was not just a rock: it was a living mountain. I felt it moving almost as if it were breathing, and I saw that all the heavenly plant-life and trees were alive as well.

I got to the door and looked in. Seeing only darkness, I began walking in. After walking several steps, the area seemed to open up into a massive circular room, resembling some kind of sanctuary or throne room. The first thing I noticed, right beside the door, was a throne to my left. I followed the thrones around the room and saw many more thrones around its perimeter against the stone wall facing the throne in the center. There were twenty-three thrones. Immediately, I knew in my spirit that they were for the seating of the 23 living letters, which entered and were seated over the course of 46 days of seating ceremonies, two days per letter.

Behind the elevated throne in the center of the room, I noticed a massive lampstand. Its fire was burning bright and large, maybe a hundred feet high. It burned with each of the colors of the lampstand in a very specific and unique layout (*see Fig. 2, below*). This was the Seven Spirits that were burning so bright that their light was streaming out of the door and still drawing me in as before.

In front of the lampstand, in the center of the room, was a larger, taller throne, made out of stone and elevated by six stone stairs. The seat and backing of the throne was red, and its arms were set with precious jewels and stones. There was One standing beside the throne as the Son of Man. He was in a long white robe, with brilliant light emanating from His Being, eyes of fire and hair that was light. He was gazing at me with intent. He said nothing, but motioned for me to come up onto the throne.

I was carefully and fearfully stepping up to the elevated throne when He motioned for me to sit down. I felt the weight of the honor of being invited to sit on the throne. As I sat, it pleased Him. I began to hear creatures, beings, and angels shout loudly as if they had been anticipating the seating of a son in this great mountain.

Seated in the throne, I looked to my left and saw a stone table next to the throne that had seven orbs, or spheres, floating over it. They looked like clouds with lightning shooting throughout them. I knew immediately that the seven orbs were the tools of the Seven Thunders. They are available to the enthroned, seated son to use in order to properly administrate and decree Yahweh's Word into the earth from that throne-seat, from the heavenly position of being seated in the mountain. As I was seated and everything shouted in anticipation, Yahshua began to ascend and hover into the air, rising up into the center of this throne room. Everything in the throne room began to scream and shake as though thunder was rumbling. As He was elevated, He began to flip and turn and spin and fold in and out quickly and more quickly and more quickly until He imploded into a ball of the brightest light I've ever seen.

When He became the ball of light, everything stopped shaking and became calm. Everyone, including me, fixed their eyes on this ineffable light descending back down toward me. As He descended as light, He entered into my chest, and His light began to stream bright out of my eyes, my mouth, my hands, and my feet. The first thing I noticed about His creative light filling me and exuding from my "body", was that I was no longer afraid, and that I no longer had permission to ask what I should do with the throne.

As a seated son in my throne room mountain, the place He prepared for me to inhabit in His house of many mansions, I was keenly aware of what I needed to do. I had the knowledge of how to use that seat of authority as a speaking place.

I began to do so with great purpose and intent as I administrated the blueprints of Heaven into my life and the world around me.

Elijah Ward

Figure 3: Throne Room Mountain (Elijah Ward)

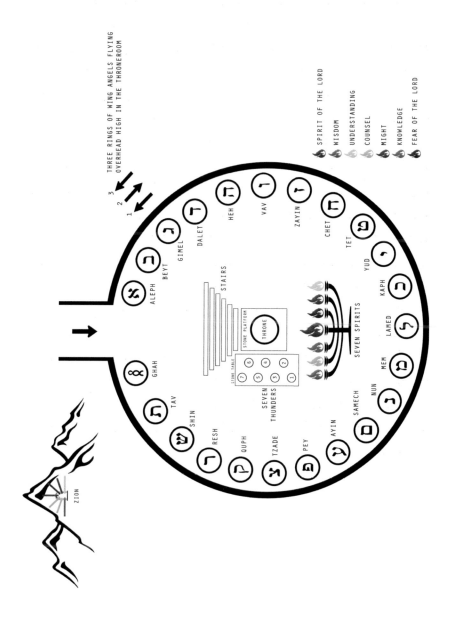

Joey Dixon's Perspective

The diagrams I make first start when I engage with or give honor to what wants to be seen. Then a vision or shape will appear and from that, it builds upon itself.

Life as we know it is basically a grid made up of numbers, sounds, shapes, light, and matter. We live within this framework and are subject to its "seedtime and harvest," or life and death. So, how can we overcome this law to obtain everlasting life? I believe my drawings show in part the very fabric of creation and a pathway to other dimensions and dimensional places.

I also believe that through these secret places you may obtain and bring into existence many things into many different dimensions. It is for each to find their path and obtain their promise. "It is truly given, but it is not just a given..."

Joey Dixon

Figure 4: A Perpetual Room of Pathways of Chayei Olam
(Joey Dixon)

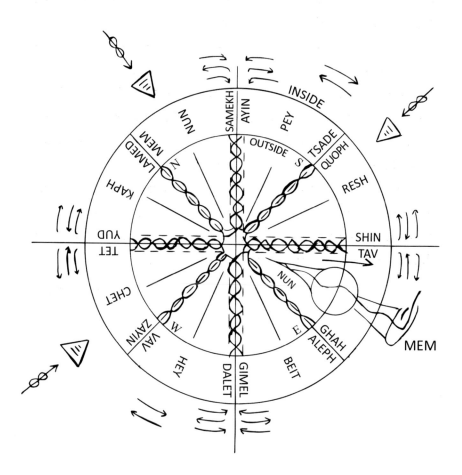

Teresa Bowen's Perspective

I am familiar with the four faces of the creatures mentioned in Ezekiel chapters 1 and 10 and Revelation 4 as the four houses of the Mazzaroth that are the heads of the remaining eight constellations or houses which represent the twelve tribes of Israel. What exactly is the Mazzaroth? "*Mazzaroth* is a Biblical Hebrew word found in the Book of Job and literally meaning 'a garland of crowns,' but its context is that of astronomical constellations, and it is often interpreted as a term for the zodiac or the constellations thereof."[51]

The main four—the Lion, Ox, Man, and Eagle—are also known as the pillars of Heaven. They are a mirror image of the heavenly thrones which Ezekiel and John saw. As the heads of their quadrants, the Lion, Ox, Man, and Eagle represent the four corners of this dimension. I believe the directions in which they camped and marched are significant for the earthly dimension and there is much more involved directionally in higher dimensions.

---

51 "Mazzaroth." Wikipedia. August 12, 2018. Accessed October 09, 2018. https://en.wikipedia.org/wiki/Mazzaroth. Mazzaroth Francis Rolleston

Table 1: The Mazzaroth (Teresa Bowen)

Faces/ Primary Direction	Houses or Tribes Represented	Traditional Constellation Names
Lion East	**Judah** Zebulon Issachar	Leo
Ox West	**Ephraim** (Joseph) Manassah Benjamin	Taurus
Man South	**Reuben** Gad Simeon	Aquarius
Eagle North	**Dan** Asher Naphtali	Scorpio

Ezekiel and John both saw the creatures with these faces. They are the cherubim that are a living part of the thrones of Yahweh and Yahshua, which reveals to us as sons of Yahweh that they also play a part with our thrones. The creatures are described in detail, from eyes to hands, feet, and wings.

They occupy specific directional quadrants, as follows:

- Predominantly out of the East: The lion face, Judah, has 3 tribes or houses attached in that quadrant, including Judah, Zebulon, and Issachar.

- Predominantly out of the West: The Ox face, Ephraim, has three tribes or houses attached in that quadrant, including Ephraim, Manassah, and Benjamin.

- Predominantly out of the South: The Man face, Reuben, has three tribes' or houses attached to that quadrant, Reuben, Gad, and Simeon.

- Predominantly out of the North: The Eagle face, Dan, has three tribes or houses attached to that quadrant, including Dan, Asher, and Naphtali.

Perhaps the four leading creatures give us a pattern of these other eight, and if each of these have four faces, then perhaps we are seeing a pattern of 12 dimensions, totaling 48 faces. These creatures and wheels are the power in which we move, seated on our thrones, through the dimensions. I can see this being the case. Yahweh always gives us glimpses into the depths of His vast creation. If we are willing to engage, then He will draw us to these deep truths for the redemption of lost truths for the leveling up of humanity to His original design.

The east gate is kept closed for the Prince to enter as seen in Ezekiel chapter 44, after the Zadok priesthood is once again established to lead us to become the priests of our God and Father, Yahweh. If we are sons, *"then heirs; heirs of God, and joint-heirs with Christ"* (Rom. 8:17).

Yahshua is King of Kings. I get this—but as sons of God, I believe we are princes, also.[52]

---

52 Ezekiel 44:3, Prince- *Strong's* H5387 - Nasiy' means King or Sheik.

Now for the four faces as the creatures, the *chai* in Eber, is the *Chet* and *Yod*, which speak of the vital force of life and this *ruach* in the creatures is described in Ezekiel 1:20 as being in the wheels. The spirit of the creatures, led by the Spirit of Yahweh, leads the wheels and His throne is thus moved.

This is the pattern in which our thrones are moved: our spirit being led by His spirit gives life and direction to the wheels, and thus we are moved through the Heavens and dimensions.

I have encountered these creatures on numerous occasions. Now I see the encounters as times we were getting to know one another so I could be ready to engage this great transportational device called *my throne*.

Teresa Bowen

The Importance of Direction and Finding the Fourth Throne Room

I'm sure you noticed, from the three different versions of throne rooms, that they were very different from each other. Teresa's version especially is different from a directional perspective. Her version is viewed from the constellations and is aligned from within the tribes of Israel. The direction of the faces were very different from the directions I see. Who is correct? We both are but it can only be discerned dimensionally. She was caught up looking from the houses of the heavens. I look from the houses of the foundations of the earth. If you do not understand the position you are in, then you will have no idea the direction you are to go. If you have not engaged the Seven Spirits of the Lord for your position and place you are to speak from, then any wrong movement could lead you to a place of nothingness. You could face an outcome that could render tragedy. If you are going down a wrong path and either out of pride or stubbornness refuse to believe the path is wrong, it could be catastrophic. Following the wrong path could cause a loss of purpose or become cyclic in nature, and thus you might never find the treasure you sought for and you might even become deaf to the sound of the Voice. Physical and even spiritual death is also possible to the lawless and rebellious in this most holy place. The latter is unfortunately realized more than one can imagine. I have witnessed this sad ending of hopes, dreams, and lives too many times. Never be afraid to admit when you don't understand where you are but you desire to understand. Always be willing to admit you've missed something so you may make a correct turn or even turn around completely if necessary. Apostle F. Nolan Ball had many sayings that I still quote. One of my favorites is "Do not despise the process." How appropriate this thinking is as we awaken to our divine purpose and the path of the progressive throne rooms.

Have you ever heard of the term *spatial disorientation*?

Spatial disorientation, also known as, spatial un-awareness, is the inability of a person to correctly determine his/her body position in space. This phenomenon refers especially to aircraft pilots and underwater divers, but also can be induced in normal conditions—chemically or physically (e.g., by blindfolding). In aviation, the term is used to refer to the inability to correctly interpret aircraft attitude, altitude or airspeed, in relation to the ground or point of reference, especially after a reference point (e.g., the horizon) has been lost. Spatial disorientation is a condition in which an aircraft pilot's perception of direction does not agree with reality. While it can be brought on by disturbances or disease within the vestibular system, it is more typically a temporary condition resulting from flight into poor weather conditions with low or no visibility. Under these conditions, the pilot may be deprived of an external visual horizon, which is critical to maintaining a correct sense of up and down while flying.

A pilot who enters such conditions will quickly lose spatial orientation if there has been no training in flying with reference to instruments. Approximately 80% of the private pilots in the United States do not have an instrument rating, and therefore are prohibited from flying in conditions where instrument skills are required. Not all pilots abide by this rule and approximately 40% of the NTSB fatal general aviation accident reports list "continuation of flight into conditions for which the pilot was not qualified" as a cause. [53]

Remember the tragic plane crash and death of John F. Kennedy Jr. along with his wife and sister-in-law? It occurred on July 16th 1999.

---

53 "Spatial Disorientation." Faa.gov or Wikipedia. Accessed September 6, 2018. https://en.wikipedia.org/wiki/Spatial_ disorientation.

On July 16, 1999, Kennedy departed from Fairfield, New Jersey at the controls of his Piper Saratoga light aircraft. He was traveling with his wife Carolyn and sister-in-law Lauren Bessette to attend the wedding of his cousin Rory Kennedy at Martha's Vineyard, Massachusetts. He had purchased the plane on April 28, 1999, from Air Bound Aviation. Carolyn and Lauren were passengers sitting in the second row of seats. Kennedy had checked in with the control tower at the Martha's Vineyard Airport, but the plane was reported missing after it failed to arrive on schedule.

Officials were not optimistic about finding survivors after aircraft debris and a black suitcase belonging to Bessette were recovered from the Atlantic Ocean. President Bill Clinton gave his support to the Kennedy family during the search for the three missing passengers.

On July 18, a Coast Guard admiral declared an end to hope that Kennedy, his wife and her sister could be found alive. On July 19, the fragments of Kennedy's plane were found by the NOAA vessel Rude using side-scan sonar. The next day, Navy divers descended into the 62 °F (17 °C) water. The divers found part of the shattered plane strewn over a broad area of seabed 120 feet (37 m) below the surface of the Atlantic Ocean. The search ended in the late afternoon of July 21, when the three bodies were recovered from the ocean floor by

Navy divers and taken by motorcade to the county medical examiner's office. The discovery was made from high-resolution images of the ocean bottom. Divers found Carolyn and Lauren's bodies near the twisted and broken fuselage while Kennedy's body was still strapped into the pilot's seat. Admiral Richard M. Larrabee of the Coast Guard said that all three bodies were "near and under" the fuselage, still strapped in.

The National Transportation Safety Board (NTSB) determined that pilot error was the probable cause of the crash: "Kennedy's failure to maintain control of the airplane during a descent over water at night, which was a result of spatial disorientation."[54]

Kennedy was not qualified to fly at night. He was confused if he was up or down due to the stars' reflection on the ocean for it was a clear night. He thought up was down and didn't trust his instruments, nor did he likely understand them. Skilled pilots say your eyes and even your feelings of what's up or down can greatly fool you in flight. Gravity at this altitude can't be felt or seen in this dimension. The instruments are usually correct because they are programmed to the gyroscopic instruments or more current GPS systems. A pilot who is not instrument rated should not fly at night or in cloud cover. If they do, horrific outcomes can occur.

The one true way that we can be assured that we will never be fooled by where we have been, where we are, and where we are going is through our constant helper, Ruach Kodesh,

---

54 "John F. Kennedy Jr." Wikipedia. Accessed September 6, 2018. https://en.wikipedia. org/wiki/John_F._Kennedy_ Jr.#Death.

aka the Holy Ghost. He must be in you and familiar with you and you with him. This comes by reason of use. We all must become skilled in our living by and in the Holy Ghost. What he is doing now is pointing us toward the Seven Spirits of the Lord. They are the tutors and governors. By engaging the Seven Spirits of the Lord and becoming skilled in the Seven Thunders, we will always understand where we are, why we are where we are, and we will never be fooled by our surroundings. Whatever dimension we are designed to inhabit will never intimidate or fool us. We will rule in righteousness from that position and place.

As we continue to engage by the Spirit and refuse to cave in to what is considered normal, then at some marked point in your process you will find the fourth throne room. This throne room is the fourth dimensional throne room and is best described as a tesseract. It is the inside out and outside in. Although I describe this throne room as a tesseract which includes the mystery and dimension of space/time, let us never forget that this room cannot be achieved but by the Spirit first. We will be skilled in this amazing place as we continue from within Yahweh and whatever face and faces He desires to speak from.

In serving as a minister for over 33 years, I've experienced many good and not-so-good situations within peoples' lives. I have been honored to be called on to be present soon after a birth and likewise greatly moved in witnessing the last breath of many. I have stood with young parents for the glorious responsibility of unfolding a newborns scroll. I have also conducted well over 100 funerals. While I was being trained in ministry, Apostle F. Nolan Ball taught me and many others the protocol and traditions for funerals. But now I believe in *Chayei Olam* and hope to never have to conduct another funeral. In almost all of the funerals I have conducted, I have read from First Corinthians 15:12–22.

> *12 Now if Christ be preached that he rose from the dead, how say some among you that there is no resurrection of the dead?*
>
> *13 But if there be no resurrection of the dead, then is Christ not risen:*
>
> *14 And if Christ be not risen, then is our preaching vain, and your faith is also vain.*
>
> *15 Yea, and we are found false witnesses of God; because we have testified of God that he raised up Christ: whom he raised not up, if so be that the dead rise not.*
>
> *16 For if the dead rise not, then is not Christ raised:*
>
> *17 And if Christ be not raised, your faith is vain; ye are yet in your sins.*
>
> *18 Then they also which are fallen asleep in Christ are perished.*
>
> *19 If in this life only we have hope in Christ, we are of all men most miserable.*
>
> *20 But now is Christ risen from the dead, and become the firstfruits of them that slept.*
>
> *21 For since by man came death, by man came also the resurrection of the dead.*

²² For as in Adam all die, even so in Christ shall all be made alive.

When the cycles of the ages were being broken in 2009, I found myself in a peculiar place. While conducting graveside funerals and usually standing next to the casket of the deceased, I would begin to describe the process of resurrection mentioned in First Corinthians 15, but I began to sense myself shifting into another place. At the time I didn't understand ages or dimensions, but I was greatly moved by what I was sensing even though I didn't have a reference point for it.

One particular graveside service was in an old cemetery. We were burying my sister-in-law's mother. As I began to speak, I felt an eruption from the depths of my being. My sister-in-law, Veronica, picked up on it immediately and began to praise Yahweh. It was so awesome! My voice began to change as I saw what was happening dimensionally. The undertaker from the funeral home looked up at me as if to say, "What are you doing and what is that sound coming out of you?" When you see something dimensional and you know you've been invited to see it, a sound comes out of you that harmonizes with Heaven and earth. I had chill bumps upon chill bumps. I began to hear creation groaning and shouting that "IT WONT BE LONG NOW UNTIL THE SONS AWAKEN OUT OF THEIR SLUMBER!" Well, the time has come and it is *now*! The sound comes from our throne rooms within us and from within Him who is in us.

I find the following scriptures are very pertinent to me and our house in this day. No matter the great mysteries revealed, they are a gift from our Father, Yahweh. It is in His love through Yahshua's blood that we find truth, forgiveness and our righteous inheritance.

> *To whom God would make known what is the riches of the glory of this mystery among the Gentiles; which is Christ in you, the hope of glory.* (Col. 1:27)
>
> *[4] But God, who is rich in mercy, for his great love wherewith he loved us,*
>
> *[5] Even when we were dead in sins, hath quickened us together with Christ, (by grace ye are saved;)*
>
> *[6] And hath raised us up together, and made us sit together in heavenly places in Christ Jesus:*
>
> *[7] That in the ages to come he might shew the exceeding riches of his grace in his kindness toward us through Christ Jesus.*
>
> *[8] For by grace are ye saved through faith; and that not of yourselves: it is the gift of God:*
>
> *[9] Not of works, lest any man should boast.*
>
> *[10] For we are his workmanship, created in Christ Jesus unto good works, which God hath before ordained that we should walk in them.* (Eph. 2:4–10)

So, let us set ourselves to rule from these amazing throne rooms in mercy, in peace, and founded upon the love of Yahweh. From these mobile thrones we will transcend time and be ready to rule in righteousness, peace, and joy in the Holy Ghost.

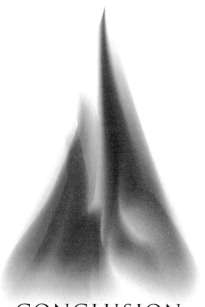

CONCLUSION

My decision to release *The Big Reveal* in two parts instead of as one book involved many deciding factors. I wanted to expedite the publishing process since writing an extensive book can take years. Finishing Part 1 has helped me to pursue the finish of Part 2. It is expedient that we engage what is required of us to be Yahweh's revealing in the earth. Part 1 is in no way a complete list of requirements and protocols to become part of The Big Reveal. That is a personal matter between you and Yahweh. But it is meant to set the bar to think differently from our slave years. In Part 1, I have meant to not only inform you but to challenge us all to think from the Christ within us.

In chapters one through six, I have touched on a few experiences and challenges of revelation that have begun to reform me back into Yahweh's original intent. This reforming has begun my awakening to my identity of being in Christ. By this, I will not only recognize who He is in me, but it will help enable me to handle the great glory I'm positioned to exemplify. By engaging His fullness, I will represent our family in the most prestigious manner of our glorious family in this amazing age that we now occupy.

Part 1 of *The Big Reveal* is a type of alignment for the glorious change into Yahweh's purpose. Part 2 is about a cause and effect from what we have become on earth and in Heaven. In Part 2, I hold nothing back in revealing what Yahweh has invited me to see.

I'm greatly honored to present to you what I've seen and heard. It is designed to challenge you as much as it has challenged me to dive or soar into what, in the last ages, we have considered the supernatural. I may sound extravagant and over the top at times in proclaiming what we will be and do, but remember that the outcome is for the glory which Yahweh has purposed. We have come too short of that glory until now, but the alignment of the ages has come and so will His glory in us who believe and engage with all of our beings.

> *And the seventh angel sounded; and there were great voices in heaven, saying, The kingdoms of this world are become the kingdoms of our Lord, and of his Christ; and he shall reign for ever and ever.* (Rev. 11:15)

Blessings to you as you engage what was, what is and what will be.

Aaron Smith

ACKNOWLEDGMENTS

To Robbie Smith, my wife of over 41 years. You remain the mainstay of my life. You are an amazing wife, mother and grandmother now to eight amazing grandchildren with another on the way. Our life has definitely been an adventure and I'm thankful. I love you.

To Teresa Bowen. Thank you for your commitment to assist us in so many things that have enabled the successes that we have attained. You are an amazing seer and communicator of the ancient secrets that are now being revealed. Thank you for your version of the throne rooms.

To Joey Dixon. Thank you Joey for being a patient seer that is willing to remain unseen as you continue down your promised ancient path. Your faithfulness and loyalty is amazing and Yahweh is ready to reveal your unique view of His mysteries. Thank you for your version of the throne rooms.

To Elijah Ward. Thank you for embracing the dimensions of Yahweh with all of your heart. I stand amazed at your daily commitment and advancement in the ancient mysteries. Thank you for your version of the throne rooms.

To Sarah Smith. Thank you for your dedicated heart to make sure that this project is of our hearts and spirit. Your work to perfect the graphics and layout are amazing. Thank you also for being the wife of our oldest son, Jordan, and birthing our three beautiful granddaughters.

To Rachel Hall. Thank you for your professional and dedicated hard work in editing my work. I know it is difficult to edit a storyteller and keep the heart but you have. We miss you guys here in Mobile and wish you all the best in your advancement.

Thank you Austin Smith. You have helped me to understand rules that I do not like within edits. You are my brilliant nephew that I greatly trust and love. Your scroll is amazing!

Want to find more revealing reading?

Check out these Scrolls of Zebulon publications:

Come Up Here: The Place of Our Original Intent
Aaron Smith, 2016

Zadok: The New... Old Order
Teresa Bowen, 2016

The Fourth Wheel Story: New Creation Man
Teresa Bowen, 2017

Friends of Eber: A Reference Guide to the Living Letters of the Hebrew Alphabet
Aaron Smith, Elizbeth R. Corley, Teresa Bowen, Y.A. Butler, and Daniel Cook, *et al*, 2018

The Everyday Awesome Adventures of the O'Reillys
Book One: The Kingdom Quest Begins
Book Two: Onward into the Mountain
Samantha Mahoney, 2018, 2019

COMING SOON

The Big Reveal: Part 2
Aaron Smith, 2019

Find them all through www.scrollsofzebulon.com

Aaron Smith founded The Rock of Mobile church, which has now been renamed Gates of Zion, in Mobile, Alabama, USA, where he is the Senior Minister. He has spoken at conferences in the U.S. and internationally, and is guest speaker with the online training base, The Nest: Where Sons Mature. He is founder of OPe technologies, a technology company inspired by scripture in Ezekiel chapters 1 and 10, and Revelation chapter 4. Aaron enjoys spending time with his family that includes 9 grandchildren.

Rock of Mobile/Gates of Zion
6245 Old Rangeline Rd.
Theodore, AL 36582
www.gatesofzionmobile.org
info@rockofmobile.org